Tough Lessons
The dark side of success.

tough
Lessons
The dark side of success.

John Borbi

Tough Lessons
The dark side of success.

DISCOVER YOUR PASSION!

John

MARCH 4, 2015

ISU ETHICS CONFERENCE

Tough Lessons
The dark side of success.

John Borbi

Collinwood Press
Farmington Hills, Michigan

Tough Lessons
The dark side of success.

John Borbi

Cover Design and Page Layout: Jessica Angerstein

Library of Congress Control Number: 2011937937

Printed in the United States

International Standard Book Number: 978-1-4507-9206-6

To all the individuals who have been, and continue to be patient with me as I grow into a better man.

Table of Contents

Introduction

Let me take you on a personal journey filled with dramatic life changing experiences involving money, ego, gambling, and excess materialism. My story takes you on a rollercoaster ride, as I started my career with nothing, rose to the top in my profession, lost it all, spent two years in a federal prison, and finally discovered the true value of life.

A few years ago I was making $0.12 per hour as a GED instructor in a federal prison located on top of a mountain in West Virginia while completing my two year sentence for a crime involving wire fraud. (This was far from the $500,000 I was earning two years prior as an investment specialist.) Being convicted of a white collar crime and serving easy days at "Club Fed" no longer exist. I was one of a handful of white collar felons serving time in prison whose harsh environment was designed to break a man's spirit and soul. Most of the other inmates were involved in some form of illegal drugs and had served time before. They understood how to survive in jail. This was a completely new experience for me and I had no idea what to expect. I grew up in a suburban community and lived a sheltered life compared to prison.

I soon discovered being in prison provided me with a choice; I could either complain about what happened to me and blame everything on someone else by becoming a victim, or I could see this time as an opportunity to admit my own personal failures and then grow, learn, and shape myself into a better man. This path was not going to be an easy one for me. I had to learn humility; let go of my lust for material items; and recognize my unhealthy obsession toward making excessive amounts of money.

Prison life allowed me to be blessed with the opportunity to face adversity while stripped of social luxuries. I had no idea this is exactly what was needed to discover my true identity, recognize what is most important, and finally value the many amazing things in my life that had become overshadowed by materialistic greed.

My two years in prison became a personal journey of prayer and self reflection and allowed me to discover my passion for life all over again.

Society teaches us to always strive to be the best and never settle for anything, and once we achieve this, then we will discover happiness and success. If we have more money, a stronger job title, a bigger house, fancier car, and more "stuff", then our lives will be complete. Right?

Unfortunately, you will begin to find "grey" areas and justify many decisions to achieve your goals and dreams. This is the biggest trap that is never exposed and eventually some individuals will fall into the dark side of success at some point along that journey. Unethical behavior becomes the accepted choice and the quest for more consumes you. There is no longer "right or wrong," there is only justification.

The story you will read helps you discover the warning signs and ways to break free from this destructive pattern, allowing you to enjoy a balanced life filled with success and passion in every area.

Chapter 1:
A young entrepreneur is shaped

People often ask me if I remember when my life started heading in the wrong direction, or if there was something I could have done differently to avoid falling into the traps I did later in my life. The short answer is, no. It has always been my personality to strive to be the best and never settle for anything less than what I am capable of. But, isn't that what society is always teaching us? The harder you work, the more success you will have and the better your life will be; right? We are not supposed to lead a life of mediocrity. That is boring and a waste of the talents we are born with. For me, planning and achieving goals to shape my future was all I focused on. I looked 2-3 years out into my future and made sure my actions in the present coincided with my goals for the those days ahead.

Even when I was in the third grade, I remember selling candy after lunch time to my fellow students to earn extra money to buy toys for myself. It was a simple case of supply and demand, and I recognized an opportunity when one presented itself. When the afternoon craving for candy hit my fellow students I would open my desk and reveal the candy on sale for the day. Sometimes I even teased everyone by savoring a piece for myself and allowing the scent to fill the classroom. That was a great way for me to advertise my product and drive others crazy. Some may call me evil for doing that, but I knew how to entice my friends into buying my product. I learned what my "clients" wanted and made sure I bought only the candy that would sell. I made sure to take care of my best clients. Even at a very young age I knew how to succeed and achieve my goals. The goals may have been small, but to an 8 year old, making $10 was all the money in the world!

As I grew older I realized having the highest grades would open doors to the future I desired. If I was not accepted by a recognizable university, then it would reduce my chances of being hired by the "right" corporation, which would reduce the potential working income I could make in my life, make it harder for me to buy all the toys I wanted and live in the big house I dreamed of, and not allow me to travel to all the places I wanted to see in the world. So, as a middle school student and high school student I made sure I studied and achieved a very high grade point average to ensure my success several years down the road and potentially the rest of my life. Hard to believe I was planning my life when I was 13 years old, but that is what I felt an achiever/ leader did. I knew if I worked hard as a teenager, then my life as an adult would be filled with success and happiness beyond my dreams, and I knew I only had one chance at this. Life was passing quickly and I could not afford to let any time slip away. I was determined to guarantee my own success and nothing would stop me.

Looking back I don't feel I went after life with a vengeance; I think of myself as a boy who knew what he wanted and worked very hard to achieve it. Was I consumed with success and money? Probably, but I was praised for my achievements and never thought I was doing anything wrong. After all, top organizations are always looking for leaders and entrepreneurs. They don't want people who strive for mediocrity or laziness, they want strong drivers and aggressive personalities.

While in high school I earned A's in my classes, participated in varsity sports, performed community service, and rounded out my resume for my college application. Everything was falling into place. I could see my hard work paying off and my plan working perfectly. I became a part of the executive council with the National Honor Society, was elected senior class president, and began working an internship.

I was determined to demonstrate my ability to handle all aspects of life at once and achieve peak performance in each of them. I would leave nothing to chance and over achieve to impress everyone. The problem was, I could never allow myself to be satisfied or enjoy the present moment. With each success came a new challenge; there was always a way to do things better or prove how much more I could accomplish if given the chance. One very important lesson I never learned, there would always be someone smarter, stronger, faster, or better than I was. No matter what I achieved, it was second to another person. However, I looked at this as an opportunity to push myself and never settle, and as a tool for growth and an incentive to become the person I desired. I felt this shortfall proved to me I could never rest on my current accomplishments because they were merely yesterday's measure of being second best......I was not willing to settle for second best!

Today's students have even more pressure on them to achieve the highest grades and live the perfect life to ensure their own future. Students are always looking for ways to cut corners and then justify their decisions. They tell themselves, if they do not maintain the highest grades, then they will not be accepted to the best universities, and then they may be viewed as failures by their parents or fellow students. They are tempted to cheat on an exam or falsify documents. They rationalize their behavior by saying it is only a grade, nobody was hurt; "I will study harder next time and not cheat again." The problem is, once they cross the line, it makes the decision to cheat easier the next time, and soon it becomes a habit.

The next phase in my life and continued quest for success moves into my college years. I was accepted into a private university and realized I had the potential to receive a very good education; I truly wanted to expand my intellect and embrace my studies. I told myself high school was merely going through the motions to achieve the higher grades and to be accepted into a good college; now it was time to really take my education seriously. The funny thing is, I always started with good intentions, yet once I moved into the next phase of my life I failed to live in the present and focused on what I should be doing to plan for the future. So, once again I justified my decisions and said, "If I can finish college in a shorter period of time, then I will begin my working career sooner and start to make money earlier." After all, what I really what I wanted was to make money so I could buy things and start to truly enjoy and live my life; college was just another stepping stone to my ultimate goal in life. I failed myself again and believed I was making the best decision; I would sacrifice now and make up for it later when I was further into my career. (As a society we always plan on doing better in the future, which allows us to justify our current poor decisions.) How many times have you thought to yourself, "I know this is not right, but I will make up for it tomorrow?" The problem is, tomorrow never comes around.

I began my studies with the plan to become an architect. I won several state level awards for my drawings in high school and was excited to learn the philosophy of design and further my knowledge of architecture. This lasted through the first semester. I remember thinking to myself, "How much money can I really make as an architect?" I began to realize not many architects live extravagant lives and make enough money to live life the way I intended. Plus, it takes a long time to work up through the system and become recognized. I had a passion for drawing, but that soon gave way to my other passion, the desire for money.

I was also a member of the golf team in college, and I remember my teammates telling me I should transfer to the business school; that is where the real money is made and a degree from there would open many doors when I graduated. That was all I needed to hear to confirm my decision about moving forward into the business program and finding a career that would push me while allowing me to make lots of money. Another passion I had while growing up was trading stocks and following the stock market. I remember using play money to buy and sell stocks for fictitious profits; I would scour the newspaper for stocks I felt were underpriced and had the potential for big price swings up. Of course, I had no idea what I was doing, but I made myself believe every stock I picked would go up and each was a stock nobody was following. (Back then information was difficult to find about a company to make an educated decision on the fair value; the internet today makes life so much easier to research a stock. Little did I know I would be making the same choices about stocks later in my professional career as an investment advisor.)

I frequently picked the lower priced stocks because I wanted to hit homeruns; I was not interested in stocks with 10% positive moves. The stock had to have the potential for a quick 30%-100% return within a short period. The thought of buying a stock for the long run, the "buy and hold" strategy was never of interest to me. I wanted the quick gratification of profit and the ability to move on to the next stock. (This attitude toward investing would come back later in life and be my downfall.)

My new career was born and I pushed hard into the school's finance program. I felt I needed to make up time, so once again I made a plan to succeed in a short period of time and adjusted my thought process. I enrolled in classes year-round in an effort to complete my degree in 3 ½ years. I had to prove my ability to handle anything and demonstrate entrepreneurial spirit, so I started a painting company to provide income while at college and understand how to create a profitable company. I also maintained a fulltime internship with a brokerage firm to learn the investment field, played on the collegiate golf team, and averaged 18 credit hours to complete my degree on my timeline. My "never settle" personality drove me to work harder than ever before and focus on the life filled with great reward just a few years away; I could almost taste my sweet life ahead! I definitely did not waste a single second in those years. I loved the challenge. It pushed me and gave me energy.

A lesson I learned from that point in my life was how I would do things to impress everyone and show them how I could handle so much. I felt, the more people who told me I could not "do it", or I was taking on too much, the more I had to prove I was better than the average individual and I could handle anything. It was never too much! Looking back, I wish I would have taken more time to enjoy the wonderful things happening in my life, but nobody could have made me believe that; I had dollar signs in my eyes and all those things needed to be completed before I could start making the big bucks.

The internship with the investment firm was a great trial by fire. It was back in the late eighties when cold calling was a necessity to gain new clients, and it was a brutal way to spend several hours of my day. I arrived in the office of a top producer who taught me the art of prospecting and selling stocks to individuals over the phone. It was all about the "sale" back then. There was no intention to determine if the stock was the right fit for the client, it was about pushing the stock of the day onto a client and then figuring out how much money was made on each transaction. (Churn'em and burn'em was a daily statetment made by all of us.)

I was also influenced by the original Wall Street movie. I watched that movie and saw myself as the young aggressive stock broker who could go out and make as much money as I wanted and then sit back and enjoy an extravagant lifestyle. My heart filled with greed and my quest for money grew exponentially after witnessing that movie. I could relate to the Bud Fox character, and felt I was smart enough to climb the investment specialist ladder without falling into the trap of insider trading or any other criminal activity. I felt I was strong enough mentally to never cross that line.

Back to the story of my internship; I would walk into the office every day, be handed a piece of paper with the hot stock or bond of the day, and then a stack of names and phone numbers to call. I called the east coast if I worked in the mornings, and the west coast if I worked in the evening. I was given a script on what to say, but I soon developed my own style and knew how to sell over the phone. Believe me, I developed thick skin in a hurry! I hated cold calling and having people hang up on me or yell at me for disturbing them at the office. I was called names and made to feel like a low-life scum many times. But, it was a valuable lesson and allowed me to discover quickly if the investment business was for me and if I could make a career out of it. The thing that kept me going was the stockbroker I worked for. I remember he always wore the best suits, talked about the amazing places he traveled, the expensive restaurants he ate at, and told tales about the lifestyle he lived. It was all so extravagant and amazing to me. I wanted that life! I specifically remember him telling me a story when he went into a store and spent several thousand dollars on clothing; to me that was incredible to be able to have that much disposable income.

Chapter 2:
Journey as a financial advisor begins

I became a licensed financial advisor in the spring of 1995 with a full financial services firm and had no idea how I would succeed in a business that has a greater than 90% failure rate. I had no clients, no natural market, and no money in the bank to pay the bills at the end of the month. The one thing I did have was a passion for investing and a tremendous drive for success. I was not going to let anyone tell me I would fail!

I started working many long hours and pushed the limits in every direction. I began my work day at 6:30am and did not arrive home most nights until 9:30 or 10:00pm. This was followed by training every Saturday and some Sundays. I truly believe you can achieve anything you desire; it is all a matter of what you are willing to sacrifice to make it. I often tell people, "Making a million dollars is easy; you have to decide what is more important though, making money or spending time with friends and family?"

At this stage in my life it was all about the money! I had goals of a big house in a golf community, an expensive car, first class travel to any place I desired, high stakes gambling in Las Vegas, eating at the most expensive restaurants every night if I wanted, and the ability to buy almost anything I desired in an instant. I achieved all of this, but paid a very high price for it when it was all said and done.

Pride and ego will drive you to achieve success at any cost and will allow you to justify any decision and blind you into bad choices.

I continued to work hard and started to build a clientele. In the beginning I wanted everyone as a client and would spend 10 hours in multiple meetings with a client who wanted to invest $1,000 in an IRA which generated $20 in commission for me. I remember other advisors asking me, "Why are you wasting your time with clients who have such a small amount of money to invest?" At this point it was not entirely about the commission. I succeeded in my own mind because I gained one more client and could prove to others I was making it in this business. Plus, I was able to look myself in the mirror and feel good because I listened to the client and placed them in an investment suitable to their specific financial goals. I wanted to make a difference in people's lives and help them grow closer to their own financial dreams. I wanted both of us to benefit and develop a long term relationship built upon trust and understanding.

I remember working 80+ hours/ week in the first year and making $24,000. (My average hourly rate was below minimum wage.) My friends could not understand why I worked so hard for such a little amount of money; what they did not understand was my long term focus. I knew in the financial world you are grossly underpaid the first 3 years, but then you are grossly overpaid as each year passes beyond that mark. Most advisors do not make it past the first 2 years. They are asked to leave by the firm because they are not making their "quota," or they quit on their own because they are not making enough money to pay their own monthly bills and survive. I have seen too many people so focused on the short term, they never get out of the "short term." If you are always trying to solve the immediate problems in your life, then you will never allow yourself to move forward and change into the life you desire. Sometimes a little sacrifice today will pay off and allow you to enjoy a much happier life longer term.

Starting from nothing was ok since I knew I had to start somewhere, and the longer I stayed the better chance I had of achieving my goals.

As each year passed, I gained more clients and continued to increase the average size of their investment. My referrals were coming in from many clients and my schedule was starting to fill up; it is amazing how simple the formula for success can be sometimes. If I did what was in the client's best interest, listened to their needs intently, and truly developed a relationship with them built on trust and long term focus, then they shared my name with other friends, co-workers, and family who were dissatisfied with their current investment professionals. My days of cold calling were almost over and my days of personal satisfaction and truly helping others were becoming the daily norm. I soon discovered people were less interested in the products I had to offer and more interested in the level of trust they had in me as an advisor to recommend the best personal strategy for them. Some advisors were so caught up in finding the latest & greatest mutual fund that they lost focus on the person who was sitting directly across from them. I found a way to connect with clients and make them feel as though they were my only client.

As a teenager I always had a passion for the stock market and trading individual stocks. When I started as an advisor I soon became more interested in the investment side of the business and was hopeful I could find a position that focused solely on the stock markets. I did not have to wait long to catch the break I was looking for. In my third year in the business I saw a real opportunity to become the Investment Specialist for the firm, as the current one moved on to a competitor. Being the "driver" type personality, I was not going to let this chance pass. I worked very hard to learn more about the markets and demonstrate I knew how to communicate with the high net worth client. It was another goal I set my sights on. I decided I would not settle for anything short of gaining that position myself!

I was given the chance to become the Specialist for a probationary time. I passed the time with flying colors and began my next phase of allowing pride and ego to run my life. Of course, at the time I congratulated myself for a job well done. I told myself I deserved the new position and that it was a reward for working extra hard. By society's measure of success, I was advancing along life's path at an accelerated rate by gaining a more prestigious title and a larger paycheck than my colleagues. As the investment specialist, I was given an override from the agency's production as well as my normal commissions from my own clients. In short, it meant a lot more money for me. But, I was told, "There is nothing wrong with that;" you should always use your skills and passions to the maximum capacity you can. Use your gifts to help others; just because you are paid a lot for that is a bonus. I could see my materialistic goals becoming a reality as I sank deeper into the dark side of success. This dark world is run by pride, ego, and a constant need for material items.

Chapter 3:
Passion becomes obsession

At this point I was making $150,000 at the age of 31, just 4 years after having an income barely above poverty level. This dramatic increase in pay would be one of the keys to my eventual downfall. I felt like I was due a reward for working so hard and sacrificing all those years before. Why not spend some of that money on myself and others around me? After all, I believed my income was NEVER going to stop going up. I'll have plenty of money coming in future paychecks. So, I began buying items and taking nicer trips. There was no need for me to be conscious of the money I spent. If you feel guilty about the purchases, it takes most of the fun out of buying things.

My rise within the company was noticed, and added to my growing ego. The more success I had, the more I needed; it was truly an addiction. I could never get enough! I welcomed every contest from the mutual fund companies and internal company rewards programs. I had to prove to everyone I could conquer any task, and welcomed every challenge they wanted to throw at me. When I failed to achieve the optimum goal of a contest, it gave me even more incentive to work harder and assure I did not fail the next time. Sometimes failing is better than always winning; it keeps you hungry and fuels your inner drive to push harder and make sure you do not fail the next time.

At this point I noticed there was literally no ceiling to the amount of money I could make, so I set my sites on bigger goals. I wanted to make $1 million dollars annually by the age of 40. At the rate I was going, I figured it would be difficult, but not unobtainable. I started to measure my life by the amount of money I made and the material items I possessed. In fact, I looked at others the exact same way. If someone lived in a large home or drove an expensive car, then they must be successful and living a wonderful life. I confused monetary success with life happiness; I did not know how wrong I was. When I drove past a 10,000 square foot house, I thought to myself, I will have that one day. I never questioned if I was going to have it, just when I would have it. (Isn't that what society is constantly teaching us? The more you have the better your life will be? Nothing could be further from the truth!)

I realized the typical clientele I met with would not provide enough commissions for me to achieve the high aspirations I set for myself and I needed to change where I was focusing my energy. This drove me to focus primarily on the ultra-high net worth clientele, and seek individuals who had at least $1 million or more to invest. Plus, these people were living in a world I wanted to become a part of; they attended all the right parties, ate at the best restaurants, and talked about all the amazing places they visited on their vacations. It all sounded so perfect, almost like a utopia that existed solely for people who were rich and were "above" the rest of society, a place where money created an escape from reality and brought nothing but fun and happiness to those who were a part of "the club".

I knew I had to create an image of success and market myself accordingly, so I decided to hire a marketing firm to develop a new brochure and a plan to put my name further before the public through media and seminars. Because my ego had grown so large, I gave the firm a "blank check" and never considered how I would pay for their services. Once again, I was willing to sacrifice the short term, to focus on the long term benefits. Investing back into "yourself" is essential to foster future growth. I saw many advisors view this as an expense instead of an investment; that is why they would always achieve mediocre growth and virtually guaranty future failure. They did not believe in themselves enough to change and think outside the box. Most people are so afraid of failure they are willing to accept mediocrity instead of taking a chance. Becoming an above average producer is much easier than most people realize; it requires you to do just a little more than everyone around you. If you are required to make 15 appointments in a week, then try making 16 going forward; that 1 extra appointment will pay significant dividends in the days ahead. I promise you will never be disappointed!

I knew I was making a lot of money at the time and would continue to make more in the months ahead so, I was willing to make a large investment back into my own business. To the marketing firm's credit, they developed an amazing brochure and put me exactly where I wanted to be. It cost me close to $100,000 to pay for all the brochures and the marketing firm's services. However, in my mind this would be pennies on the dollar relative to the commissions I would generate in future years. If this helped me make my commissions goal of $1 million dollars annually for the next 30 years, then spending $100,000 to create $30 million is a great return on investment. This was one of my early mistakes, and warning signs of how irrational I had become. I felt I needed to have whatever I wanted and I would not let anyone tell me I couldn't; I justified every decision and blinded myself into believing I always had the right answers and knew exactly what would work perfectly. My pride and ego consumed my thought process and made me believe I was better than most advisors, and smarter. All I had to do was earn more money and things would take care of themselves. I started to create my own fantasy world where failure did not exist and money would always be there to bail me out or make the problems disappear. If I failed, then I would take a trip to escape, and then tell myself how successful I had become, which allowed me forget about my failures.

One of the ways I created more exposure for myself was by hosting investment strategy sessions for the ultra-high worth investor. (An ultra-high net worth investor was an individual with at least $1 million dollars of liquid investable assets, not including real estate. This number is much higher in today's dollar equivalents.) I knew how to communicate with this market, and realized how to create interest. I had a 45 minute presentation about how I managed portfolios and different investment strategies that were specific to the ultra-high net worth investor, and finished my session with a great close. Individuals who typically have that much money want to become part of a specific group, so I knew I had to provide this for them. I told my audience how I only manage money for 100 clients. This was my first "hook". Once you take something away from someone, then they typically want it, or want to be a part of it. Some of those investors sitting in that room now wanted to know how to be in my top 100 client list. The second part of my "hook" was by taking it away from them. I made a very arrogant statement. I said, "When you come into my office, I am going to interview you. I will determine if your money is good enough for me and if you are the type of client I want to allow into my top 100." Can you imagine the ego and arrogance I possessed to say something like that to a group of investors who always had investment professionals begging for their business and pleading for a chance to take over their portfolios?

The thing was, it worked. When I wrapped up my session and walked to the back of the room, I became surrounded by people asking to schedule an appointment with me ASAP. I had one individual who said, "John I have $12 million in another account; let's meet tomorrow morning so I can transfer it to your firm."

The marketing strategy worked and I started to gain clients who had more than $1 million to invest. I felt like the ultra high net worth market was all mine, and I looked like a genius. (Of course this only added to my own self confidence and growing ego.)

Once again, my success only added to my future downfall. I continued to climb the ladder in the company and now ranked in the top 1% in the nation for annual commissions. In fact, I was asked to speak at many regional and national conferences to teach other advisors how I achieved success so quickly, and how to cater to the ultra-high net worth market; a market everyone wanted a piece of. I loved going to these conferences, because I was treated very well and relished the praise I received from other advisors. This fed my ego and reaffirmed in my own mind I was on the right track to future greatness. In my mind, I felt like I was actually helping others lead better lives by teaching them how to make more money and buy more "things"; in essence I felt was giving back to those who needed my help. (I created the illusion I was doing a good deed.) I loved the spotlight, and it gave me another item to add to my list of accomplishments; it also gave me the chance to meet other top producers and learn from them.

One thing I never lost sight of was the fact there would always be someone smarter than me and someone who knew how to make more money than I was currently making. So, I asked lots of questions and absorbed their wisdom like a sponge. My mentor taught me to always ask others for their help; most people enjoy helping and the feeling it generates. The other benefit of interacting with top producers was how it humbled me. It taught me I was far from the "biggest fish," and I had a long way to go to catch up to their sizable earnings. The reality was I could not compete against a top advisor whom had been in the business for 20 years; I could not defeat the power of time and their years of experience.

Now just a short 6 years into the business I was at the top! I achieved most of my goals. My income was $300,000+ at age 33; I helped drive the agency to number 2 in the company as the investment specialist; I was still in the top 1% in personal production; I had respect from my bosses and other top advisors; and I was building the house I dreamed of. Life seemed to be perfect. Little did I know what was around the corner.

The stock market correction of 2001 was in process. This is when the NASDAQ lost over 50% of its value and the "Dot Com" bubble would burst. Up to that point, making money in the stock market was very easy. Investors had become spoiled with excessive returns and everyone thought their annual returns should be 20% or higher! Day traders were buying and selling stocks without even knowing anything about the company, all they were concerned about was how quickly they could "flip" the stock for a profit. I remember doing the same. I would buy and sell a stock in a matter of minutes, make 30%, and then move on to the next trade. It was a crazy time and nobody believed it was out of the norm. Investors believed the glory days would never end and always wanted more; all sense of traditional trading methods disappeared and logical thinking about the reality of this unsustainable growth was not present. I fell into the same trap and began believing I was such a great stock picker/trader that even if the stock market had a correction, then I would find the companies nobody else was tracking and maintain higher returns for my clients. After all, I foolishly thought I was much better than my actual abilities.

At first, when the market started to have its downfall, it was a blessing for me. I had the "do it yourself" investor realizing they needed to seek professional advice, and I had as many appointments as I could handle. My referrals were coming in more and more as the "home trader" began losing more money and started to panic about their losses; of course I took advantage of their fear and created an environment of a professional trader. My office had computer screens flashing stock charts and real time trades, while CNBC played on a television to complete the office display. I wanted a new prospect to walk into my office and feel comfortable transferring their money to my management. I wanted them to realize they made the right choice and I would earn my commissions while generating higher returns with each year that passed. Plus, I knew each new client I gained was a potential source for referrals and future clients. It was the best way to ensure growth within my business and maintain my focus of reaching my goals and desired income of $1 million dollars annually.

My income continued to climb and passed the $400,000 mark! Unfortunately, my patterns of spend now, and save later were firmly entrenched into my lifestyle, and I was spending money faster than I could make it. My life of excess was growing larger and larger and my quest for material items and need to show everyone around me how successful I had become was out of control. I would drink $100 bottles of wine at home as my "everyday" wine. When I hosted small parties or had friends over I would purchase expensive flights of wine and spend $2,000-$3,000 on a couple bottles because that was another way for me to show how people with money "did things." I became a very welcomed customer at the wine store, and was treated with tremendous respect. (Another ignorant attempt on my part to pretend to be someone I was not, and foolishly believe I understood wine enough to be respected. The store owner saw me as an easy sale and was happy to sell me lots of expensive wine.)

I ate at the best restaurants, spending $300-$400 on a meal without hesitation, or ordered gourmet carry out several nights a week because I was too lazy to cook. I loved eating exotic foods and experiencing a world of extreme cuisine that money allowed me to enjoy. When a new high end restaurant opened, I had to be there immediately to try it. Not necessarily for the food, but more for the ability to say I had eaten there if one of my clients brought it up in conversation. I wanted to always be one step ahead of everyone else, and create the sense I was a part of their world and always shared something in common with them. Also, as strange as it may seem, it was another way for me to offer advice to them; it is part of the illusion created. They could ask me anything and I would hopefully have the answer for them. I did not want to be one dimensional to my clients, and was happy when they saw me eating at the same restaurants they were, or attended the same theatrical performances. I worked very hard to have a presence at the "right places" around town. Little did I know how much harm this was doing to me as a person and the false sense of happiness this created. I made myself believe life was getting better. In reality it was getting worse, as the dark side of success began to overtake my life and run it deeper and deeper into chaos and emptiness.

My favorite city to visit was Las Vegas. I flew there 4-6 times a year and always stayed in a suite at the Bellagio, and was comped for everything. This environment gave me the perfect escape from reality and permitted my fantasy of being treated well to be fulfilled every second I was there. Life was amazing in Las Vegas. I could go to a 5 star restaurant, order a very expensive bottle of wine and eat an incredible meal – all for free. When the bill came, all I had to do, was sign it, because everything was comped from the high level of gambling I did each trip. I remember ordering a massive lobster and eating one quarter of it, and throwing the rest away. The lobster alone was probably $200. What a waste of money and abuse of excess! I would have a $500 bottle of champagne waiting for me at my room upon arrival to toast the beginning of my trip.

I played golf at Shadow Creek golf course when only invited guests could play there. When I arrived the head pro personally greeted me as I exited the limo and assigned me an individual who took care of my every need while there. Prior to my play at the course, they asked me what kind of beer I liked to drink so they would have it iced for whenever I desired it. I could be in the middle of a fairway and request a beer, and someone would be there within a few minutes to bring it to me while I played. The level of service was beyond amazing! They made sure I did not see another person while I was golfing; they wanted me to think the entire golf course was mine for the day. When I was warming up on the range, the caddy was watching my swing and flight of my shots very intently. I had no idea this was going on or aware of what he was actually doing while I warmed up. I later learned he was marking the distances of each club in his head and learning my specific style of play. On the first hole I asked him the distance to the flagstick, before he told me the distance he handed me a golf club. I asked him for a distance again, he told me to hit the club he chose fully. By the third hole I realized he knew exactly how far I hit my shots and I stopped asking for a yardage. I just waited for him to hand me a club and tell me, hit it "full" or "take a little off it." This caddy was incredible, and added to my personal experience. Their intent was to make this a golfing experience of a lifetime; Shadow Creek accomplished this task very well.

Of course, all of this world class pampering came with a price. I would typically gamble $30,000 in a weekend at the Bellagio and never think twice about it. I was under the impression my income would never stop and it would only continue to rise as the years passed. My game of choice was craps. I loved the excitement of watching the dice roll and bounce off the wall to reveal the number I wagered on. I was so driven, I needed the high energy of a craps table. The noisiest and most exciting area in a casino is the craps table. When someone was on a hot roll I would high five the person next to me and gave the biggest smile possible; all sense of reality was gone at that moment. It was all about living in the moment of winning money and having fun; there was no stress from work or concern about obtaining my goals. It was pure pleasure for me.

I liked to share my winnings as well. Once, I was part of a great roll and had a lot of money spread across the table, I told the person rolling the dice I would pay her $100 every time she hit one of my numbers. She did not believe me. The next roll she made was one of my numbers, so I tossed a black $100 chip across the table. She was so excited that she became more focused on rolling my numbers instead of her own. I think she walked away with $600 in tips from me. It was fun for me as well - I probably made over $10,000 on that roll.

There were times when my pride and ego revealed itself as well. One time I walked by a craps table which had 5 mature gentlemen playing, smoking cigars, and having fun. I glanced at the table and they gave me the look as if to say, "You are some punk kid who can not afford to play with us. Why don't you run along and find a table with a smaller limit and stop bothering us." Being as arrogant as I was, I could not stand for that insult, and even if I lost all my money, I was not going to let them get the better of me. (Pride always steps in and justifies many poor decisions I made during those years.) It was a $100 minimum bet table, which means every bet you make must be $100 or greater. Since I like to play four numbers plus a pass line bet with odds, I was risking around $800 with every single roll of the dice. A person can lose a lot of money in a hurry on a table like that. But, I was bound and determined to show them! I stepped up to the table and checked in $10,000 to play with. Their eyes lit up and were very surprised I was willing to risk that kind of money. I was clearly the fool at the table though. These gentlemen could have been multi millionaires and losing $10,000 to them was like losing a few pennies. As it turned out we all had a great time playing together and I was very lucky to break even on the session. My foolish pride could have cost me a lot of money that night.

My twin brother was married at the Bellagio and I remember a couple of stories from that trip. On his wedding night, after the ceremony and dinner was completed, we all returned to the Bellagio for some gambling. I wanted to spend a few moments alone gambling with him and enjoy the environment. We went to a high limit blackjack table and sat down.

I wanted to make sure nobody else sat down at the table next to us, so I asked the pit boss if she would reserve the table if I played $500 hands and my brother played $25 hands. She was happy to oblige as I asked for a $10,000 marker and we began watching the cards dealt. I had no idea how to play "proper" blackjack, but it was more important for me to spend time with my brother laughing and having fun than it was if I won or lost money. We played for probably 30 minutes and I lost around $5,000; I think he may have won. When we left I passed the game War, the same game I played as a kid. I stopped and played $100 hands on a game that has no skill whatsoever. I was just so intrigued by the game I had fun with as a child that I had to waste some money reliving my younger days. I switched to $500 hands occasionally and attracted a crowd of people as they were amazed to see an idiot like myself gambling so much money on a simple flip of the card. I wasted a lot of money gambling, but I definitely had a lot of fun too.

I was generous with my money off the casino floor as well. One time when I checked into my suite at the Bellagio, a bellman helped deliver my bags. I had already gambled before I checked in, and had some loose chips in my hand. I went to tip him for his services but did not have anything smaller than a $100 bill in my money clip. So, I reached into my pocket and tossed him a green $25 chip as a tip. He was so excited and could not thank me enough. For me it was just a chip and had no real value, but to him it was a huge tip. He proceeded to share with me how he and his wife were saving to buy a house and how much he appreciated my generosity. I made his day and he valued every dollar he made that day. I was the complete opposite and did not value anything and wasted money every minute.

Like any addiction, I always wanted more and needed a bigger challenge. My trips to Vegas became more extravagant and my average bet increased every time. I look back and think about all of the money I wasted gambling, it makes my stomach churn about the excess and waste when so many people needed food, clothing, and shelter, yet I chose to not help them. I was so selfish and only concerned about myself.

(I still love visiting Las Vegas, I think it is an incredible city and I am excited every time I walk off the plane. I just have a significantly smaller amount to gamble with now and I am the one hoping some high roller will tip me for a hot roll of the dice.)

Many times I was my own worst enemy, after all, my pride and ego told me I was "the best," so no matter what happened in my life, I thought I was smart enough to discover a way to make it better or I was lucky enough to change any misfortunes that came my way. For example, one time I returned home from a trip to Vegas after a losing weekend. This was quickly forgotten though, when I received my two week paycheck for $44,000! Once again, I was so blind to the reality of life I was not making rational decisions and living in a fantasy world that seemed to have no end and only continued upside with more money at every turn. I was living in excess and justifying my materialistic lifestyle without concern for the future or proper retirement planning or saving. A prudent person would have lived a comfortable lifestyle on $100,000 and saved the rest for a rainy day; that was never a consideration for me. I was a young man making all that money and filled with compliments from those around me. I remember a manager who introduced me to a group before I spoke stating, "It is not a question of if John is going to make $1 million in a year, it is a question of when." How is that for filling my pride and ego?

In my mind if I was going to save for the future, then I would have to alter my lifestyle and not eat out as often, gamble as much, be forced to travel less, and take away from all the fun I thought I was having. Pride and ego thrive on excess and zero restrictions; they feed your mind with the false sense of pleasure and prevent you from taking an honest look at yourself and the pitfalls that surround you or wait in the days ahead.

Chapter 4:
First dose of reality

One day a new investment product was introduced and an incentive was announced to entice advisors. The bonus was going to be $30,000 for every $1 million dollars sold/invested. The wheels in my head started turning as I posted it on my wall and recognized it was just a matter of time before I received my bonus. I became very focused on that money and knew exactly how I would spend it. I went on the internet and looked up the price for chartering a private jet for the weekend to take myself and a couple of friends to Las Vegas for the weekend. The price was $28,000 for a nice sized jet. Perfect! That was the exact motivation I needed to show off my latest accomplishment and tell everyone I no longer needed to fly on a commercial jet. I moved up in the world and now fly on a private jet - my ego was out of control. As I mentioned earlier, greed becomes an addiction and your mind seeks bigger and better events and items; I was no longer content with what I had and it was never enough. I thrived on the rush of accomplishing things beyond what others thought were possible, and I wanted to shock them. I never wanted someone to tell me, "You can't do that", or "You can't have that."

A short time after my crazed fantasy about flying on a private jet, the first thought of reality and humility hit me. I started to think about how ignorant it was to spend close to $30,000 on an airplane ride and possibly waste $30,000+ gambling, when people are starving in communities close to me. I was willing to waste $60,000 over a weekend!! I recognized I had finally gone off the deep end and gotten out of control in my spending and obsession with material items and quest to demonstrate how successful I was to those around me. I started to think for the first time that I should be thankful for all I have and donate that money to a group in need. The first chink in my pride armor occurred.

I began to wake up to all of the waste I had created over the last few years and recognized I needed to change my life. I was a man making a lot of money, but not making a difference in this world. I remember thinking to myself; I am a shell of a man who is measured by income and material items; not by deeds done to better society and those around me. How did I allow my life to fall so far off course and make so many mistakes in life? (I did not know my worst decisions were yet to come.)

I wanted to rethink my life and start to change how I lived it; this is much easier said than done. I craved a sense of balance in my life and wanted to return to the point where I simply enjoyed helping people and did what was right instead of what would make me look best. I lost my way on life's journey and was not living His plan; money and material items had become the focus in my life and serving the Lord was a distant second.

I put together a financial plan for myself and decided to cut back on all my expenditures, save for retirement, and donate a lot more to charity. Unfortunately, others had become dependent upon me and were not willing to change their standard of extravagant living; they would not let me slow down and make less money; they too had become accustomed to spending without limits or concern for the future. Even my bosses felt I would be wasting my talents if I cut back on my client base, so my pride and ego won out again and I began to fall back into the dark side of materialism and greed. I was too weak to say no and make the much needed lifestyle changes. People have come to me and found it hard to believe I could not just walk away from everything. After all, I recognized how it was destroying my life - why didn't I end it sooner? The problem is, when pride and ego consumed my heart, there was no room left for humility. We have all witnessed others around us who have lost their lives to addictions or poor decisions, and wondered why they did it. I am not making any excuses for my actions; I alone made those choices and was tenacious in my efforts to achieve all my materialistic goals. I craved it and would not stop at anything to gain it, so I deserved the emptiness that came along with it and take full responsibility for the pain I caused myself and so many others.

Let's go back to my story and the chain of events leading up to my worst decision yet. The stock market continued to fall. That did not deter me for a second, as I was so filled with pride that I built myself up as an advisor who could beat the market. What an ignorant statement to make. I looked at this as another challenge - one I could defeat with my perceived expert skills and knowledge of the financial markets. I was always seeking out new challenges and ways to prove to myself and others that I could handle and defeat anything I was given; nothing was too difficult. As I mentioned before, ego and pride will help you make ignorant decisions and fall right into a deep hole. Plus, that was another sign of my addiction - I had to have higher highs; the challenges and rewards always needed to be bigger. (It became a reckless, self destructing thrill of the chase.)

Chapter 5:
Crossing the line, the point of no return

Soon I would take the biggest step in my downfall and start down a path that had no return. I would finally face my biggest challenge - myself.

As some clients started to lose money with the fall of the stock market - which is a completely normal result - they would call me and wonder why their statements showed a loss. (They were foolishly led to believe by me this would not occur. In my prideful acts they were told I knew how to position assets in a portfolio to minimize or eliminate losses.) Instead of recognizing it was ok to lose money in a down market, I told them I would work harder and discover stocks that would make up for their losses and discover investments other advisors were not smart enough to find. I convinced them next month's performance would be above expectations and they would be pleased; pride was in full swing at this point. I was not willing to face myself in the mirror and admit I was not nearly as smart as I thought I was. If clients were realizing losses, then I must not be this great stock picker or investment specialist I claimed to be. I needed to face the reality of my life and recognize perfection did not exist; all along I figured if I worked hard enough I could achieve perfect success and happiness. If I could pretend to have a perfect life with the items I owned, the vacations I experienced, and the money I made, then my pretend life would eventually turn into a real life. (I believed the cliché - "Fake it until you make it".) Somehow I achieved what I thought was a perfect fantasy world, only to wake up one day and realize I actually created a world of chaos and self destruction. This fantasy world quickly became my own prison filled with emptiness, loneliness, unhappiness, and personal numbness. I felt lost and had a complete lack of control, which was very hard to admit since I always felt in absolute control of my life up to this point. I became so good at fooling everyone else that I even fooled myself.

My world was spinning out of control and I was no longer doing what was in the clients' best interest, I panicked and did anything to cover my mistakes; I started to fall into self-preservation mode and tried to find a way out of the mess I created. My pride kicked back in and I told myself to get off the self-pity train and use my stock picking skills to get back on top! Pride and ego are fierce and don't just leave your heart quietly; they keep coming back and wait patiently for the perfect time to emerge and bring the sense of hope or a solution to the current threat. Every time I thought I was becoming a changed man, I would fall back into my old bad habits and have to fight another internal war to escape the materialistic world I craved for so many years. I even thought I could control my own greed and use it to my advantage to pull me out of the abyss I was falling into. Once again, I was naïve to believe I could find balance between the two worlds and use the dark side just long enough to make life better, then abandon it and lead a life filled with passion for helping others. (Looking back I shake my head at how smart I thought I was, yet how ignorant and foolish my decisions to control life actually were.)

I began to make big buys on small stocks to make up for losses, hoping I was making the right choice in individual stocks; I never thought the stock market bubble was about to burst and I would be right in the middle of it. I was accustomed to buying stocks and making money on almost every trade; the market could not do the complete opposite, could it? Unfortunately, it could and did. For every 1 gain, I had 3 losses. I told myself I could not believe a person who was as smart and good at stock picking as I was could not beat the market;

again a statement made with enough pride and ego to fill a football stadium. My ego continued to convince me that only losers quit! I am not a loser and I will not quit! This is just a minor setback and I need to be confident in my abilities and experience. Other advisors were dropping from the industry and times were getting tough very quickly. I told myself I was better than those guys, and this was an experience I needed. I imagined I would look back on these turbulent times and smile for making it through without giving up. So, I dug my heels in and prepared for a battle I was not willing to lose; I put together a short term investment strategy and moved forward. I made huge individual stock purchases looking for a $1 dollar positive move. Then, I would sell, make a profit and inch my way back to a positive return. I knew this was a huge mountain to climb, but I also realized the only way to reach the top was one step at a time; I could not make this in one single leap. A problem occurred when my strategy did not work and the stocks I picked lost money. I was now in real trouble and my worst decision was just around the corner.

A good client of mine had a friend who had $50,000 to invest and asked me to help her friend manage her portfolio. I was not interested in such a small portfolio, and did not see any benefit from adding this client. I was still seeking clients with portfolios larger than $1 million dollars, definitely not the pittance of $50,000. My client convinced me to manage her friend's money and I took her on as a client. I remember thinking to myself this could turn into a real opportunity. If I could double her money with the right stock picks, then I could prove how good I was at turning a small investment into a large sum in a short period of time. My plan started out perfectly and the portfolio grew to $70,000; my ego kicked in and I became greedy looking for a "home run" stock. I invested her entire portfolio into one stock. I knew the risks and monitored that stock very closely, determined to sell after it made a profit and rose in value. The stock began falling and I became emotionally attached to it in hopes it would stop falling and start trending higher. I convinced myself it was a short term hit, and if I had a little faith in the stock, then I would be rewarded in the long run. (Technically I knew better than this. If a person becomes emotionally attached to a stock, then they always sell when it is too late and lose more than they should. I never listened to my own advice.)

The stock continued to fall in value as I fell deeper and deeper into my own emotionless pit and felt zombie-like. I was no longer making rational decisions about anything in my life, and could not distinguish right from wrong; my life was not about rational decisions anymore, it was about justifying my choices and plainly moving forward. I lost all control and started to just go through the motions of life. It sounds like another cliché, but I remember looking in the mirror and wondering how my life had fallen so far out of line. I no longer wanted to be the person I had become or desired the success I worked so hard to achieve. I reached a point in my life I never dreamed was possible; I did not know what my future held. Up to this point I always had a plan and knew what my life would be like in 1 year, 3 years, 5 years, and so on for the rest of my life. Now I had no ambition or drive to achieve victory over my next challenge and honestly was anxious for this rollercoaster of highs and lows to end.

The clients' portfolio had fallen to $35,000 with the stock losses and she needed her original $50,000 to purchase a condo. Of course, I lost all the money she needed and my pride and ego would not allow me to tell her the truth about the losses. I had some tough choices to make. I could write a check out of my own portfolio for $15,000 to make up for her loss, which I was willing to do even though it was illegal. The problem with that choice was I could be setting a precedent for paying off other clients and drain my own bank account. Another option was to be honest with her and tell her of the loss and that it is one of the risks of investing in individual stocks. The problem with that choice was that I would have to admit I was not as good a stock picker as I thought. I was not willing to do that out of fear of losing other clients and their potential spreading of rumors about my inabilities to manage money wisely. The last option I considered was a little more complicated, but I felt would be the least detrimental to everyone and save my reputation in the process.

I had a client who was worth $40 million dollars. I did not manage his entire portfolio, but I had a piece of it. I justified my illegal thought process accordingly. He lived a very modest lifestyle and basically did not want to spend his money, nor did he want to look at the monthly statements he received. He trusted me with his money. I thought this was the perfect solution to my "problem". I could merely transfer the $15,000 from one client's account to the other client's account, and then reposition a few investments to generate a higher rate of interest to make up for the "transfer". I could then invest the wealthy clients' portfolio back into the original investments and he would never notice the transaction. I thought I was so smart for coming up with a solution where I did not have to admit my poor stock picking choices. The other client would receive their $50,000 to buy their condo, and the wealthy client did not use his money anyway, so it would simply be a short term loan until the higher interest paid him back and he was made whole again. I told myself this was a perfect solution where nobody got hurt and nobody noticed. The state of mind I was in was complete disillusionment and justification; it was about survival in a world where the walls were closing in on me and I had no idea how to stop it. Nobody knew what was going on in my life or had any idea how far off the deep end I had fallen; I continued to put up a front of how perfect my life was and how I managed everything in harmony and success. Yet, inside my own world nothing was working and all I saw was complete failure. I even fooled myself many days just to avoid the reality of how bad things were.

So, I decided to transfer the money from the wealthy client's account into the other account. That was technically stealing and considered wire fraud, a federal crime. I justified this by saying I would work really hard to replace the money I "borrowed" and get back into the normal investment strategy. As I forged the client's signature, I remember asking myself, "What are you doing? If you get caught you will lose everything." Little did I know how true that was and how much I wanted that to occur. This was going to be the ultimate battle within myself between the false life lead by pride and ego, and the real life lead by humility and responsibility. Pride is very strong and that dark side of me knew if this battle was lost then life would come crashing down instantly.

When I forged the client's signature in my office, I felt numb and completely lost in my own world. I knew what I was doing was wrong, yet I could not do anything to stop myself. I remember it was later in the evening and the office was empty. There I was, all alone, committing an act that would change my life forever and turn my world upside-down. I did not feel too nervous. I convinced myself this was the best choice and proceeded with my plan. I was wearing a custom tailored white business shirt with the top button undone and my tie loosened slightly; my shoes were shined and I looked like a hard working professional putting in extra hours to stay ahead of the other advisors. I don't know what a person looks like who is committing a white collar crime, but I looked like a "normal" employee taking care of business.

I walked out of my office and headed toward the fax machine; I double checked the transfer amount and the signature to make sure everything was correct. I took a deep breath and asked myself if this was what I really wanted to do, because there was no turning back after I crossed that line. I only hesitated for a second before I punched in the number on the fax machine, and then fed the paper into the slot. I waited for the confirmation and felt a sense of relief once the act was done. At that moment I broke the law and committed wire fraud. It seems like a harmless act, but it started a chain reaction in my own life that would cause many people pain and sorrow over the next few months and years.

When I faxed that simple piece of paper I did not think much about how I was breaking the law. I stole from that man in a quiet and unthreatening way. I justified my own behavior by telling myself, "It is not like I went to his house with a gun and caused him mental or emotional trauma." But, I hurt him in a much more devious way and took advantage of his trust in me. The truth is, I may have been worse than a man with a gun.

Part of my justification was my ego telling me that, even if I do get caught, things will turn out okay; after all, I am a top producer, they would never fire an advisor making big money for the agency. That was a very ignorant and arrogant statement to make; it shows how far from reality my mental thought process truly was at the time. I figured I may receive a "slap on the wrist" if my forging was discovered; I never thought in my wildest dreams what I did would be worth 2 years in federal prison. I did not see myself as a criminal or threat to society at the time; I needed to take a closer look at myself and realize I was not above the law, nor should be treated any better than anybody else who broke the law; I deserved to go to prison for my actions. Those are the cold hard facts!

Looking back, I can say that was my intention all along. I was too weak to quit on my own, so the only way out of my dark world was to commit a crime that left no choice but banishment from the industry without questions or negotiation, and removal from society until I figured out how to become a contributor to those around me, not a detriment. I no longer desired success or looked in the mirror at the shell of a man pride and ego created; I did not want that reflection any more. Therefore, I committed internal suicide to kill off the dark side of me and give the responsible side of me a chance to be reborn and grow again.

It is kind of ironic, that according to society's measure of success I was a man who created the perfect life. That year I would make $500,000, live in a house worth three-quarters of-a-million dollars, drive an expensive car, have the ability to purchase anything I desired, travel often and stay in 5 star hotels, have two wonderful children, and be 34 years old with nothing but upside in the years to come. Yet, I hated the person I had become and wanted the ride on the dark side of success to end. I worked all my life to achieve the goals I set when I was merely a teenager. I finally obtained everything I desired, but it became a life that cost me so much more than any item I ever owned; it cost me the things that don't have a price and can't be bought and are so much more important - a sense of peace, love, and balance that warms a man's soul and fills his every day with passion. That is truly what I craved and desired.

Chapter 6:
All sense of reality is gone

You would think that would be the end of the story, but it was not. My pride and ego were not going to give up that easily, and they rose to the top once again, as I convinced myself I could hide this "transaction" and get back on top without anyone noticing. I remember wondering if the client I stole money from would notice the transfer out of their account? I knew he received a statement confirming money was withdrawn from his account, and another monthly statement that showed the account balance and any transfers or transactions during that period. I sweated it out for 30 days wondering if I would be caught. My mind was racing and trying to create a story I could use as an excuse in case the transfer was discovered. I remember not sleeping much and being consumed with anxiety, wondering if I pushed myself too far this time. (I remember the mind games I played and panicked feeling of the unknown. They were worse than how I felt after I was caught.) I created and suffered a torture that exceeded anything I experienced before, yet I continued to put up a front to everyone else that my life was perfect. Nobody recognized the stress I was under. I aged greatly over the next few months as I was committing my crime.

The wealthy client did not open their statements, and the transfer was not discovered. I breathed a huge sigh of relief, and at first thought this was a good thing, as I had escaped my unethical action. (In truth, it would have been better if I would have been discovered then.) My stress level went down, I was able to enjoy life again, and I thought I was given a second chance to learn from my poor choice and never repeat it. Finally, the mental feeling of my world crashing down all around me disappeared, as I experienced a sense of relief and felt like I got away with my poor decision to steal money. I vowed to never do it again. That lasted a mere two weeks. Little did I realize I was only in a state of denial and temporarily created a false sense of peace and hope to allow my mind and body a chance to recover and prepare for the next wave of criminal activity. We all know how far we can push ourselves before there is a complete breakdown; I discovered that "ledge" and turned away from it just in time. But, it did not take long before I returned to that place and leaped off into a dark pit of despair and loss of reality. Soon the line between right and wrong was gone and I made decisions without any concern of consequences for my actions.

Once I crossed that line and inched further and further into the dark side of ego and greed, criminal activity became a part of my life; I no longer questioned whether I should or should not do it, I just stole more money and made the decision as easily as I made most other decisions on any given day. I realize this sounds absurd to most people, and you are correct - it was insane! I crossed the line so many times, at the end of my embezzlement days I was so far from the original line I created, I had no idea my life had fallen so far off the edge. Looking back, I am thankful I was focused on one type of criminal activity and did not branch off into other destructive behaviors such as drugs or acts of violence. (I am not minimizing my actions. What I did was terrible and hurtful to many individuals, and it never should have taken place.)

Once I was able to get away with my first act of stealing, then it made the next one easier, and easier, and easier, etc. A couple of clients called and were concerned the market was declining and wanted to know if they should sell their stocks and be more conservative. I told them that is what they are paying me for, to beat the market - another ego driven comment and mistake. A prudent advisor would have listened to his clients and rebalanced their portfolios into a more conservative style and managed the money wisely. But, I was not listening anymore - I was more interested in proving how smart I was. "Pride always comes before the fall." This quote described my life perfectly at the time.

Guess what? My great stock picking abilities turned out to not be so great in a rapidly falling stock market. As the market fell, I needed to cover more losses, so I figured if I got away with stealing once, I could get away with it again. Most clients accepted the losses in their portfolios as normal market risks and never expected me to cover those losses; I was my own worst enemy. I solely decided to transfer money into their accounts. I could not deal with the thought of having them say I was not a good advisor and have them move their portfolios to another firm. I honestly felt I was one of the best and should never lose a client to anyone else. (I realize how irrational and absurd this thinking is, but at the time I was not thinking or acting clearly.)

Over a period of 7 months I "transferred", (in reality I stole and re-deposited), over $500,000 into various clients' accounts to keep up the appearance they were not losing money in the stock market and I was a "great" advisor. Most clients just looked at the total account balance to see if they gained or lost money. When I made a deposit into their account, many of them did not notice, and were content as long as the bottom line was okay. It got to the point where I did not even question what I was doing, forged a document without hesitation, and then waited for the money to show up in a client's account. At one point, I remember sitting in my office dumbfounded at how quickly I lost all sense of values. The difference between right and wrong was blurred beyond distinction and nonexistent. Yet, I still felt I needed to keep up the charade and appearance of a top producer as if life was still "perfect." I was able to justify any decision I made - another problem and characteristic with the dark side of success. I believed there was no right or wrong, there was only justification.

Meanwhile, as each day passed I became more and more disgusted with myself as a person and recognized the many mistakes I made in the past several years. I became a parasite feeding off of society and only taking things beneficial to my own life and not giving anything in return. I wasted so much money over the years that could have helped feed and clothe others. I did not need any of the "stuff" I collected, shoved into closets, and typically forgot about, but at the time I felt like I earned those items and treated them as rewards for all of my hard work. I should have used my skills to teach free basic investment strategy sessions and help others understand the stock markets; I had plenty of money and should have donated anonymously to local groups, or offered my time in whatever capacity it was needed. I felt like I wasted several years of my life I would never be able to get back.

I lost all my enthusiasm and passion for investing and was not interested in contests anymore. I remember as a teenager combing through the news paper trying to find the hidden company nobody knew about, and then buying their stock and watching it rise in value. When I was in college, I recall watching CNBC and being glued to the ticker as it scrolled along the bottom of the television. I would spend hours mesmerized by the symbols and the values as they passed my eyes. As technology and the internet grew, I stayed up late into the night researching companies and other stock markets to recognize trends and predict the best investment strategies needed to take advantage of the information I compiled. I truly loved investing and was hungry for more knowledge every single day! It is amazing to me how all of that passion could disappear; I never thought that was possible and expected to be involved with the stock markets throughout my entire life. It was just another massive price I had to pay for my poor choice of letting pride and ego control my life and consume me. It truly is very sad.

Another sacrifice I am ashamed to admit was my false relationship with God and Jesus. I believed I had a relationship with them and understood the path I needed to take in life to fulfill His will; how wrong I was! Looking back I can see the signs, but always felt like I had everything under control and would never let things get out of hand. I feel like God was tapping me on the shoulder saying, "John, you may want to step back a little and pay attention to what you are doing with your money and life." Of course my response was, "Don't worry; I have it all under control." I think we had "conversations" like this often, as He let me slide deeper and deeper into my own hole, yet I kept brushing things off and always felt like I could walk away at any moment if needed. I had no idea how out-of-control my life was at that point, and how complicated my world had become. I know I was never alone and He was/is always with me. Finally, He had no choice but to let me fail, take my life down several notches, and remove me from the materialistic world I created. There is no question I placed money and material items ahead of my relationship with Them and asked for forgiveness many times for that. I will share later in my story how thankful I am for failing and allowing Him to build me back up again; they were very hard lessons to learn, but I was too stubborn to learn any other way.

Some sanity and reality crept back into my life and I realized it was a matter of time before my "transfers" were discovered and my life would come to a screeching halt. Some days I welcomed it so I could have this burden lifted off my shoulders. I finally got my wish.

The client whom I made the most illegal transfers from was moving his portfolio to another firm. At this point I had no morals left and could not make a sound decision if my life depended on it. I knew he was moving his account and I wanted to make one more transaction, so I transferred $70,000 out of his account. This was the straw that broke the camel's back. When the new investment firm received his account, they recognized it was short $70,000 from the amount they were expecting. They called me and asked for a copy of all recent activity, and noticed the recent withdrawal. I panicked and told them it was a reporting error and the money must have been transferred into another client's account by mistake. I was trying to figure out how I could transfer that $70,000 back into his account, but the money had already been split up and distributed to other accounts and could not be recovered. Imagine the immense stress I had at that moment and terror consuming my every thought.

Of course they did not agree with my answer, and needed to see proof - within hours the shortage would be wired over to their account. My heart was racing and my life was flashing before my eyes about the shame I would soon be facing. I knew this was the moment of truth and my stealing spree was coming to an abrupt end. As I started to realize the finality of this turn of events, something strange started to happen. Can you imagine what was going through my mind at that moment? Strangely enough it was a sense of peace and relief.

Finally, the life I created and no longer desired was coming to an end. I could stop running and trying to prove how successful I was. I could let events develop on their own and not feel like I had to control them or attempt to manipulate the outcome; I could just let life be. I sat in my chair and looked out into the office area as I watched other agents go about their day like they normally would; my life changed in that moment and nobody knew it except me. I looked around the inside of my office at the awards hanging on my walls and the pictures of places I visited sitting on my desk in front of me; all of this would disappear and I finally realized the value I placed on them up to this point meant nothing. Life changes in an instant and we never see the change coming, but those changes allowed me to become a better man in the days ahead. It forced me to realize the meaning of my life and gave me the opportunity to start over if I chose to. All of the money I made and the items I owned suddenly vanished, and clarity was right in front of me - if I walked down the path that opened up.

Now that a red flag was raised by the client, management immediately began looking into the transaction and recent account activity. The client's attorney called the compliance department and demanded answers and threatened to call the FBI. Pandemonium began to break out between my office, the compliance department, the general agent's office, and the home office investment department. Everyone wanted to know what was going on. Rumors began to circulate among the other investment advisors and staff within the office. I was called to answer questions, and continued to maintain my innocence to buy time and pretend it would work out. All I was trying to do was escape into my own world and wished I could fast forward and avoid the next part of my life. I always had the answers to problems and solutions to keep my life moving forward, yet this time my mind was empty and blank. It became apparent to someone at the home office that I was not telling the truth, and the compliance department and my boss began to meet behind closed doors without me. They came into my office and took the client's file from my drawer and requested any other material I had regarding his account. I am amazed at how quickly things happened and unraveled. In just a few short hours my life was turned completely upside down.

My boss called me into his office where several top managers and compliance officers were on a conference call. Then, I was asked point blank if I had stolen the money or was involved in illegal transfers with anyone else. Once again, my heart dropped and the shame I felt was immense. Most of the people standing in front of me or on the telephone were my friends and people I had known for several years; how could I face them? I believe most of them were hoping there was an easy answer and I was not involved in any criminal activity. They did not want to be forced into prosecuting me and taking the next step against me. I was too weak and scared to admit my actions at that time. Without question I was a coward and could not take responsibility for my own criminal acts and the pain I caused so many individuals, including those standing right in front of me. I can-not explain how low I felt and how disappointed I was in myself for letting so many people down; it saddens me to this day.

After I left the office I began to plan an exit strategy, knowing it was just a matter of hours before charges would be brought against me and I would be fired from the firm. I went back to my office and closed my door. I did not want to talk to anybody; I just wanted to be alone to wallow in my own misery. The day was almost over and the compliance department was researching every little detail and transaction of the clients' account. They convinced the attorney to give them more time, and by the next morning all answers would be available regarding the missing funds. I was no longer involved with the discussions and everyone knew I was the individual who had stolen the money; now they just had to track down the transfers and prove it. I remember waiting outside of my boss's office and overhearing an individual say, "He stole that money."

I started to come to grips with the reality of my situation and slowly realized the best thing I could do was to admit my guilt and move forward. It was after 6:00pm and most of the agents and staff had left; the office was quiet except for the people working in the compliance department on my case. I went to see my office manager and asked her if she had a few minutes, I wanted to talk with her. She was happy to listen and told me she knew I was not to blame for this error. I had known her since I started in the business; she had seen me rise from a struggling advisor into a top producer. I sat in a chair, put my face into my hands, let out a big sigh and told her I had stolen close to a half million dollars and was going to jail! She could not believe the words coming out of my mouth, and was shocked to say the least. I told her I would not be seeing her or anyone in the office anymore and fully expected to be in a jail cell the next morning. The only thing I could think about was the image of Bud Fox, from the movie Wall Street, being led away in handcuffs in front of the entire office.

I told her to not call anyone or share the news about my crime - I wanted to confess everything to my bosses and take full responsibility for my actions. I imagine 30 seconds after I left her office she was on the phone with someone; it would be so hard for her to keep startling information like that to herself.

I went back to my office, looked out my window, and contemplated my next action. I remember it was a cold rainy day as I stood by my desk and thought about everything. Reality continued to settle in, and I needed to focus on my personal life now. I knew what I had to do next. I needed to call my wife to tell her what I had done. I remember exactly what I was wearing - a custom-made three-piece-suit with a French cuff shirt and cufflinks; I can remember that day like it was yesterday. I told her I had embezzled money and we would lose everything. She thought I was playing a joke on her and did not believe me. Reality quickly set in for her though. Because of my selfish actions, I hurt many people along the way and I was too weak to seek help; I learned many things about myself that day and started my own process of stripping away the layers that had built up over the years.

I fully expected to drive home that night and see a police car parked in front of my house. I remember turning onto the court I lived on and slowly approaching my house looking for a vehicle. It was dark outside, so this added to the intensity of my situation. Fortunately, the street was empty and no police car was there. I parked my car on the street and just sat there for a few moments as I pondered how I would face my family. I felt full of shame and embarrassment. I finally gathered enough courage to go inside and start the next phase of transforming my life. It was hard to walk into this beautiful house I worked so hard to gain, knowing it would be sold and all the possessions inside would disappear with it. I truly had many internal battles; part of me recognized these were only possessions and meant nothing, but another part of me was still attached to these items and did not want to part from them. I had a long road ahead of me to release the power material items had on me; the best thing I could do was to be completely removed from this "world" and learn to live life with nothing and discover how wonderful life can become without materialism. (Prison provided the forced escape I needed from these items.)

That evening I called a very good attorney and tried to figure what tomorrow would be like. I still had no idea what to expect or when I would be going to prison; frankly, I was scared at the thought of being incarcerated and hoped I would receive probation and would not face jail time. Yet, I knew deep within my heart, jail would be the best thing for me and was the harsh environment I needed to be broken down to my core enough to begin building a new foundation for my life and somehow become a better man for myself and my children. As much as I wanted to be a coward and not face my punishment, I realized the only way I would change my life was to stop running away from responsibility and start accepting whatever consequence I deserved for my poor decisions and actions. How would I ever be able to face my children and teach them to be responsible if I could not do it myself?

If I want to lead by example, then I needed to start immediately! I began my new thinking process of living one day at a time and focusing on the moment instead of worrying and being consumed about the future. I had so much unknown in my life at that moment. If I worried about what the future held or might be like, then I would not be able to function on a daily basis or get out of bed. Imagine all I had on my mind - I was going to jail, but did not know when or for how long. I would be forced to sell my house, but when, and where would I move? I would be divorced, but when and how "messy" would it be? I will be gone from my children and how will I explain it to them? I no longer had an income or career - what will I do to pay my bills? How do I face my neighbors and family? There was so much to think about, and I still had to sort out my own mind and life personally. Why did I commit the crime? What kind of man am I? How will I start life over again? Is society better off without me?

The next morning I went to the office around 4:30 am, before anyone arrived, and cleaned out my office of personal belongings. I brought a few boxes and packed them full. I did not take any files or change anything on my computer, I knew the "game" was over and hiding anything at this point was useless. Plus, I wanted to confess to everything and make their life as easy as possible when they began sorting through my office. It took me an hour or so to finish everything, and then I took one last look out my window and around my office. It was a very sad moment for me to realize I would never be returning to that space, and all of the clients I helped over the years and watched grow would be told I was a criminal. I would be judged by some and forgiven by others. I developed friendships with many of my clients and hated to see it all end abruptly. I knew I would not be able to contact them and tell them personally how much I enjoyed their company and experiences. This would be another example of what I had lost. Money and material items could always be replaced, but respect and friendships were lost forever, and that hurt. I learned that lesson the hard way and will never forget it! I view life differently today. I value people and friendships on all levels. It makes me feel amazing when I smile and receive a smile in return. I know then that I made a positive impact on that person's life, even if it was only for a few seconds.

As I was leaving my office, I took a look at all the other cubicles and offices and wondered what would happen that day. I shocked everyone and changed their lives; hopefully others would learn from my greedy motives and re-examine their own lives and make changes to avoid making the same mistakes I made in life. I knew some advisors would step right into the dark side of success and view my firing as an opportunity to claim my office and go after my clients. Greed is a very powerful thing and will always make people do things they regret later in life. It may feel right at the time, but sooner or later your action will consume you and destroy some aspect of your life, even as you find a way to justify your decision.

My final act in the office needed to be completed; I left a voicemail message for my boss explaining I was the one who stole the money, and gave him the name of my attorney. I remember when I was leaving, a young agent was arriving around 6:15am eager to start the day. Flashes of my early days passed before me as I wondered if he would fall prey to the dark side of success as I had. He acknowledged me and told me to have a good day. I told him I would probably never see him again. He gave me a look of confusion as only I knew what I meant at the time.

Over the next several weeks, I met with representatives from the investment company I worked for, the SEC, the FBI, and the U.S. Federal Prosecutor's office. I told each of them about the crimes I committed and the hollow life I was leading. I spent hours upon hours answering questions and reassuring them I was the only individual involved, and there were no other crimes for them to discover in the future. They were very concerned about finding more illegal transfers, and had to assume this was bigger than what it actually was. After they completed their due diligence and were satisfied, then they could move forward and formally charge me. I had mixed emotions during those Q & A sessions; on one hand I was very thankful to "come clean" and share my story, but on the other hand, it was very humbling and difficult to admit all the poor choices I made and all of the pain and destruction I caused. The experience was very cleansing and allowed me to feel better about myself, because I was taking responsibility for my actions and accepting whatever punishment they were going to give me. But I also had to face the reality of the evil person I had become and honestly look at what I had done. It was not a pretty picture and

I could no longer sugar-coat it or pretend it was not that bad. I could not talk my way out of this one or convince others to view it in a better light. The facts were the facts, and I needed to face that. The people sitting across the table from me were not concerned about my awards, how much money I made, or any good deeds done; they separated out the personal side of things and merely wanted to know, "how I did it, and why I did it." Without question, I do not want to go through that ever again.

My life was filled with uncertainty during this discovery phase by the prosecutors, and I always wondered what the next day held for me. Up to this point I always had my life planned out. I had goal plans for every year going forward for the next 20 years. This new reality was very unfamiliar territory. It was another difficult lesson I had to learn; I continued to discover how to live in the moment because I was forced to. I could not focus on the past, because then I would never escape it and move forward with my life or start the healing/rebuilding process. I could not focus on the future because it was filled with much uncertainty and far too many questions that did not have any answers. Plus, the future is always changing, so any energy I spent predicting the future would be wasted and take away from my ability to enjoy and live in the present. Step by step I began changing my life; I felt like a baby learning how to crawl again. I had to go slow, I could not rush things even if I wanted to, as things had to take their own shape in their own time. I learned so many valuable life lessons during this time in my life. It is when life is most difficult when we learn the most and shape ourselves into becoming better people. Of course, when we are going through this shaping phase we want it to end, but at some point we can always look back and see the benefits from hardship. It is exactly what I needed.

I finally finished all my meetings and then waited for the results. While I waited I tried to settle the rest of my life; I needed to establish some normalcy. The house was sold and most of the material items with it. A new house and neighborhood provided me a fresh start and separation from the previous lifestyle. The uncertainty of not knowing when I would be charged and begin my prison sentence made life very difficult. Every morning I woke wondering if my attorney would call and tell me he had a court date. Every night I would pray for closure and the desire to move on with my life. Without question, I suffered every single day while I waited for an answer. This punishment in some respects was far worse than my time in prison. I had to wait two years for them to officially charge me! I waited, and waited, and waited; it was like a slow and painful death for me. I deserved some suffering, but wished the process would have moved along a little quicker. I could not go out and find a new job/career because I knew I would be leaving for prison soon, so I started my painting company back up and painted houses to provide an income. I was not afraid of hard work and being my own boss, and this job allowed me to plan my schedule around any court meetings, as I knew I could stop working any time I needed. This also gave me the opportunity to find personal time. When I painted, I worked by myself and could be alone with just my own thoughts. I did not have all the distractions of office noises, I could just "be." This was the beginning of my own personal path of discovery and started my next phase of asking the hard questions of myself and taking as much time as necessary to answer them. This was also a prelude to the massive amount of alone time I would be given in prison.

Another casualty of my crime was the loss of my relationship with my father. A day after I left the office and was fired I called my dad and told him what I had done. I told him specifically what had happened in hopes my honesty would bring us closer in my desperate times. Instead, I was met with anger and frustration. He told me I made the worst mistake of my life; that I was useless, and would never amount to anything ever again. "You pissed your entire life away and have nothing to live for." I was surprised and felt let down. I tried communicating with him several times while in prison, but I always received the same response. In one letter I explained all the changes in my life and how much I wanted to begin our relationship with a clean slate. He responded that I would never change and always be the same self centered man he knew.

I made a choice at that moment to not listen to his words, and recognized our relationship was over. Unfortunately, a couple years after my return from prison my father committed suicide. Neither one of us created the opportunity to bridge our differences and seek forgiveness to start fresh again. It was a sad ending to a very strained relationship.

Chapter 7:
Prison life awaits

Fast forward two years. I received a call from my attorney stating he had a court date and we would finally be moving forward with the case. I remember walking into the federal court and feeling nervous. My heart was pounding, my stomach was churning, and I was sweating through my shirt. I spent the last two years trying to forget the crime I committed, the pain I caused those individuals, and the embarrassment and shame I felt from my actions. I had to relive everything all over again as I walked in front of the federal judge and described in detail my crime and the remorse I felt for the decisions I made. It was a rush of gut wrenching emotions as I remembered how awful a person I was at that time and how regretful I was for my actions. I wanted to convince the judge that the person she was looking at now was a completely changed man and nothing like the man just described. She needed to know I learned my lesson and would never repeat those poor behaviors. Of course, none of that mattered; the facts were clear and punishment needed to be handed down. I needed to pay my debt to society for the crimes I committed and did not deserve any special treatment. That was clearly one of the worst days of my life - not because of my sentence, but because in that moment I truly realized all the mistakes I made and the terrible person I was during that phase of my life, consumed by greed and material items. I could not have felt worse about myself.

Based on the amount of money I stole and the length of time in which I stole the money, the judge was given a range based on the federal sentencing guidelines of 30-34 months in prison. Whether she thought I was a "good–guy", or a "bad-guy", it had no bearing on her final decision. I was sentenced to 30 months in a federal prison, and began serving my time in August 2004. Immediately after sentencing I was escorted out of the court and into a jail cell. The federal marshal closed the jail door and I stood there in my custom suit wondering what life would be like from this point forward. He proceeded to process me by giving me a drug test, taking my "mug shot", finger-printing me, adding my name to the bureau of prison's list of prisoners, and completing my bond. Reality set in, and I began a new phase in my life's journey.

At this point I was not scared to go to prison. I knew that was what I deserved, and I was ready to pay the price for my crimes and poor decisions. This was the first step toward recovery for me; owning up to my failure and assuming responsibility for my actions. I have seen many people over the years blame everyone else for their problems and never enjoy life going forward because they cannot get past their own issues because they don't admit to them and correct them.

I posted bond and drove home with a sense of closure. I knew how long I would be gone from my children and when I would return to them. This gave me the opportunity to finalize some details of my life before I departed for prison, and allowed me to begin to move forward. I received a letter shortly after sentencing telling me to report to a federal prison in West Virginia, about 8 hours away from where I lived, in August 2004. I immediately tried to discover information about this prison, but did not gain much knowledge. I still have that letter and will keep it as a souvenir, along with other prison items, to reflect back on the thoughts and feelings I had with each piece.

With each passing day, I experienced extreme highs and lows of emotion and understanding. Some days I would feel a tremendous sense of peace because I knew the sooner I began this next phase in my life, then the sooner it would end and I could begin another phase once I returned from prison. There were days when I could not wait to leave "society" and escape into the seclusion of prison. I knew that environment would grant me a place where I could be alone and avoid facing the shame I felt as I looked at my children and others. In prison I would not be dealing with the daily routine of paying bills, planning meals, advancing my career, shopping for groceries, driving in traffic, dealing with family issues, etc. I would be removed from a lot of the typical stresses we all face. If I did not want to do something, then I did not have to; I would only be responsible for me and control my own decisions. This sounds like a selfish act, and it probably was, but I needed to be selfish and discover myself and answer so many questions I had deep within myself before I could change and become a better man. If I did not take this time to make some core changes, then I would not grow as a person and I would not be able to be happy and at peace with my own life. I believe if you are not happy with yourself, then it is almost impossible to please and be a positive part of someone else's life. All you are doing is pretending to be happy, and sooner or later that will turn into frustration and resentment in some form. I believe, If you are truly happy and at peace, then that strength and emotion will flow from you and into the lives of all those around you. Take a moment and look at whom others gravitate towards; is it the person with the positive outlook and continued sense of understanding and desire to improve life, or is it the person who is always complaining, blaming others, and is never satisfied?

My days were also filled with sorrow and anguish knowing I was going to a place that was completely separated from my friends and family. The life I lived and understood was now being replaced with uncertainty and restriction. I remember tucking my children, ages 3 and 5, into bed at night, wishing I could hold on to that moment and bottle it up and take it with me. I knew as each night passed, it brought me closer to the night I could not be there and they would miss me. If you are a parent, then you know the exact feeling I am describing that breaks your heart. But, it also allowed me to realize how special each moment with them was. Most parents go through each day following a routine that makes time pass so quickly they never realize how precious their life and time can be when they share it with their children. Now I was able to cherish my children's smile and the sounds of their laughter; it was amazing all the little details I noticed and all the simple things we did that became special bonding experiences for us. I had a new appreciation for life as a parent and understood the most important gift I could give them was my time and love, not the money I made or gifts I thought they needed. Those items faded and eventually ended up in the trash, but the memories we created will last forever in their hearts and brought us closer together. When we realize an "end" is coming, then we approach life differently and establish a new set of values and principles. I knew my time was short and it helped me grow into a better father.

Finally, my day of departure arrived. I remember hugging my children, kissing them, and feeling my heart break as I climbed into the car knowing they would ask for me and I would not be there. How do you explain to a 3 and 5 year old what was happening? You can't. They had no concept of time and no idea about the crime I committed and the reason for leaving them. This was another form of punishment for the selfish acts I committed. I deserved this and needed to feel this pain to bring a harsh dose of reality into my life for the choices I made. Serving my prison sentence in many ways was the easy part; it was all the other personal sufferings I dealt with that really hurt me. As the car pulled away, tears rolled down my face knowing the pain I caused them and would cause them over the next two years. My heart ached like never before.

I arrived at the Federal prison in Morgantown, West Virginia ready to self-surrender and begin my sentence. I thought I had changed in many ways and became a better man over the two years while I waited to go to prison, but when I climbed out of the car and looked at the prison fences in front of me and the prisoners walking around in their khaki uniforms, some of my old defense mechanisms surfaced and I reverted back to survival mode. I looked at my time in prison as just another contest, and I had to prove to everyone that I could beat this contest and win; I was not going to fail! I figured I was too smart to be taken advantage of and I definitely would develop a plan to survive and thrive behind those prison fences. Little did I know I was walking into a world beyond all sense of normalcy and logic; a world removed from "typical" society standards and one I was not prepared for. My arrogance came roaring back into my life and I told myself, "I can beat this! Nobody is going to control my life except me!"- I still had a lot to learn - my life lessons and transformations were only beginning and the next two years of my life would be spent being broken all the way down to my core with much mental and emotional pain.

To prove I did not recognize reality yet, please imagine this scene: I have a picture of me standing in front of the prison with my now ex-sister-in-law on one side and my ex-wife on the other side of me with tears running down their faces, because they recognize I am walking into prison and will be dealing with an environment that is designed to break me. What do you think my face looked like? I did not show any emotional breakdown or concern; my face was filled with a big smile! Who walks into prison with a smile on their face?! It just shows I felt I could beat anything thrown at me. I said to myself, "How hard can this be?" I needed a healthy dose of reality, and little did I know, I was about to receive it.

I walked up to the guard shack at the entrance and notified him I was reporting on my scheduled date and was prepared to begin serving my sentence. As I walked through the heavy metal prison doors, my life would be changed forever. The guard who processed me was going to let me know immediately I had crossed the point of no return, and the world I just left was nothing like the world I was walking into. He viewed me as some suburban white collar prisoner who needed to suffer some hardship immediately. It was like he had a chip on his shoulder against anyone who appeared to have "money," or had an easy life up to that point. He was going to take me down a few notches. He immediately went through the normal routine of finger printing, conducting a drug and alcohol test, and taking my picture for my prison ID. He then proceeded to strip me naked and place me into a jail cell for 2 hours to prove he could do whatever he wanted and I would have to take it. It did not matter whether I liked what he was doing or not, this was his jail area and he controlled me! I went through a thorough strip search, and he verified I did not have any contraband or other controlled substance on or inside of me. This was the most humiliating experience I ever had in my life. All sense of personal value and confidence was taken away. I was treated like an animal in many respects. To further his point, I spent a total of 5 hours sitting in a jail cell by myself without any interaction. He made sure I realized I had plenty of time to do absolutely nothing "inside". There are no deadlines, no agendas, no places I needed to be at, and time was going to tick away ever so slowly. I was on his time now and he was going to tell me what I was going to do, how I was going to do it, and when I would do it. He maintained total control over me.

He was not done with me yet. He proceeded to take my personal belongings and placed them into a box which was then labeled and shipped home. This was done to prove his point that, "They will learn to forget about you while you are in prison." His next step was to assign me to a living space; he would have fun with this one. I was sent to the roughest unit and into the roughest wing of this unit. He wanted me to feel threatened and scared by the other inmates with whom he believed would "eat me alive." Most of these inmates had been in prison before or were serving longer sentences, so they were already a part of the prison society. I of course had no knowledge or understanding of how the system worked, so this became trial by fire; I would either learn how to survive or be taken advantage of quickly. To add further insult to injury, the guards put all the "newbie's" through an initiation the very first day. A new inmate does not receive standard prison clothing upon arrival, they receive a different color shirt and pants. The following day the inmate reports to the laundry department to be issued pants and shirts like everyone else. This lets all the other inmates know when a new prisoner arrives and what he looks like. As I mentioned, this guard was not done with me yet, he proceeded to issue me pants and a shirt that were 2 sizes too small for me. I had to walk across the prison yard and into my unit looking like some sort of freak wearing skin tight clothing. You can certainly figure out what type of message he wanted me to send. It was not funny and only made my transition into prison life that much harder. I felt humiliated in front of all these other men. This was the time I needed to fade into the background and be unnoticed, not stand out and have attention drawn in my direction.

My first night in prison was a bit unnerving. I was given the top bunk on an old worn out mattress, a scratchy blanket and no pillow to sleep on. My feet rested on the end of the steel framed bed and it was the most uncomfortable thing I had ever slept on in my life. Without question, prison is designed to house a man, not make him comfortable. They achieved this goal in almost all areas of prison life. I probably slept a total of one hour that night. I was never comfortable and it seemed like I could hear every little sound in the entire prison. The guards are required to count the inmates three times throughout the night. They use this as an opportunity to ensure all inmates do not get a sound sleep. They accomplish this by jingling their keys as they walk by and count. It took me many months to figure how to block this noise out and sleep most of the night. When I arose in the morning I realized this would be my home for the next two years, and I was devastated as

I began recognizing all the comforts I took for granted every day.

All in all, I am happy to say I survived my first 24 hours in prison and my walk of humiliation across the grounds. I also had a bit of good fortune fall in my direction as well. Somehow word had spread that a "Wall Street" guy had arrived. I was not from Wall Street, nor did I ever claim to be from there, but they knew I managed money and that was all the other inmates were interested in. They loved to swap stories about money, and wanted to be a part of that world. This helped me because it gave us an instant bond and a reason for the other inmates to communicate with me. Once they realized I was not a friend to the guards and I could be trusted, guys looked out for me and made sure I was treated fairly. This does not mean life was easy, it just means I could walk around without constantly anticipating aggression from another inmate. (I always kept my eyes open and felt prepared for the situation to change in an instant though; I never let my guard down. I saw too many guys attacked when they least suspected it.)

My first few days in prison were spent understanding how the system worked and learning all of the rules, both written and unwritten. The unwritten rules and codes the inmates followed were far more important than the guidelines posted by the guards. The guys around me helped me understand some of the rules, and other rules they let me learn on my own through failures and consequences. I also had to wait to be assigned a job. Everyone has to have a job in prison. It is not something you can decline. It takes the system 3-4 weeks to catch up with you, so I spent a lot of time hanging around all day observing others in an attempt to learn what to do and what not to do.

I also remember sleeping many hours during the day. It was like I could finally catch up from all those years of sleepless nights and refresh myself. I felt exhausted from all the stress I created over those years and this gave me the opportunity to escape reality in one respect - I did not have to answer the phone, take care of the children, work, pay bills, or be responsible for what would typically happen on a given day; I could just sleep, read and relax. This sounds like an easy life, but believe me, you get bored with it very quickly. Plus, I am not including all the other stresses prison life brings as well. The multiple counts by the guards throughout the day, the scheduled meals and waiting in lines for almost everything, the interaction with personalities that are unpredictable and often bizarre, the slop they called food that had to be eaten in order to survive, and the inability to do anything you take for granted every day, such as driving a car, going to a movie, walking wherever you desire, opening up the fridge to grab a snack, watching television, going to the bathroom by yourself, wearing a different piece of clothing, and my list could go on and on. Take a few moments and think about what you did and the people you interacted with in the last 6 hours. Prison takes things away, and made me realize very quickly how wonderful my life was, but it also helped me realize all the things I could live without. I no longer needed my "stuff." I learned to live without it, adapted, and became thankful for what I did have.

A quick side note: My career is now in public speaking and during my speeches, I often ask the audience to raise their hands if they feel they are "running the rat race." Of course, most of the audience raises their hand. My next question is; "Have you ever met anybody who ever won the rat race?" We all know the answer is "no." "If you never met anyone who won, then why are you running the race in the first place?" Why push yourself toward a finish line that is always moving further away from you, and one you will never reach?

We place a certain value on things and believe they are needed possessions to help make us happy. Ironically, they are items that may actually prevent us from achieving and enjoying peace and happiness. My life was filled with material possessions for many years, and I always made more money so I could buy more "things," yet it is impossible to stop the introduction of newer and better "things." The moment an item is purchased, it instantly becomes replaceable by the next greatest thing. We are constantly chasing something we can't catch. We are caught up in a race we can't win, but we keep trying and drive ourselves crazy in the process. Trust me, I tried to reach the finish line many times, and the harder I tried, the more consumed I became with it and the more sacrifices I made along the way to find this utopia.....it does not exist!

Prison was the only place that could teach me this lesson. I needed to be in a controlled environment where I could not go to the store and look at what I wanted to purchase with my next paycheck, or just buy something because I had an impulse and thought it would make me instantly happy. (This is always a temporary high that leads to a letdown soon after.) That was not an option in prison. It was very difficult at first; I felt like an addict going through withdrawals. In prison I was allowed to shop once a week, and the items available for purchase were primarily food items and snacks. Plus, there is a set spending limit and the space within my locker was quite small, so I had to manage my purchases wisely and only pick the items I needed for the week.

This experience taught me discipline and helped me realize how little I needed to survive and be happy. At first I felt deprived and constricted because I was not able to do what I wanted to do. I was accustomed to having things done my way and on my terms. The harsh reality check was perfect and shaped me into a better man who grew less dependent on "stuff." I also learned how to ration my food over a seven day period. If I gorged on a snack, then I had to suffer without it and wait until my next shopping day to replenish my stock. I know it sounds strange to say I suffered without my snack, but it was those little treats that helped me smile and forget on some days. The comforts you take for granted every day when you walk into your kitchen were nonexistent for me; I valued those little escapes.

My first exposure to the physical side of prison came within the first week of my sentence. A gang fight broke out about 10 feet in front of my living space. One inmate from Detroit, had a lock in a sock as his weapon, and another inmate from Washington D.C, had an iron swinging from the cord as his weapon of choice. These two bloodied themselves in a fierce battle which lasted 10 minutes, but felt like it lasted an hour. Both of them had to go to the hospital and be stitched up to seal their wounds from this intense brawl. I was absolutely in awe of this confrontation and could not believe my own eyes! I had never witnessed such physical brutality, and was frankly shocked two people could have such hatred toward each other that extreme harm was the ultimate goal.

I remember thinking that this was not happening; am I really seeing this? What makes this even more unbelievable was the reason for the fight. It was all over a "peel off." That means one person takes his shirt off and flexes his muscles in front of the other guy to show he is stronger and in superior physical shape to the other person. This move was done in front of the other guy's buddies, and it was meant to embarrass him. It achieved its purpose. In order to save "face," this person had to retaliate and start a fight to prove he was not going to take that, and he was the superior male. So, they beat each other silly all because one person took his shirt off. How stupid is that?! All sense of logic and normal human behavior according to a functioning society was nonexistent in prison. Guy's made their own rules, and there were many days when I scratched my head in utter disbelief. I still look back at some of the fights I saw and can't understand the dramatically different life that exists behind those prison walls. Without a doubt it is a world I was not prepared for, nor could anyone ever prepare me for; I just had to witness it and experience it.

There were a few reasons for the fights in prison beyond physical domination and show of brute force. Some guys liked to be involved in fights because if they were hurt seriously enough, then they were escorted off the prison grounds to the local hospital. To them, this was a way to temporarily escape prison and see the outside world. Even if it was just for a few hours, it meant freedom to interact with "normal" people and eat "regular" food if they were lucky. As I mentioned, prison takes so much away from a person that they are willing to go to extremes to get back a small taste of what they lost or had before they came to prison. I realize this is hard to believe, but it happens every day, and guys huddle around an inmate to hear his stories about the food he ate or the pretty nurses he saw and talked with. It is the simple things at that point that mean so much in life when everything else has been taken away. The other reason some inmates fight is so they can be shipped to another prison; they want a change in scenery. Imagine if you have a long prison sentence, you would get bored. You don't want to spend 10 years looking out the same window or staring at the same grey block wall. So, fighting provided a solution to the boredom and allowed opportunity for a new location and change of pace, so to speak. Again, I realize this does not make sense to most people, but it is the mindset that exists in prison and another example of a world that has its own set of rules and is completely separate in many ways from "normal" society standards.

The first 30 days in prison seemed to take an eternity to pass; hours felt like days, and days felt like weeks. I spoke with another inmate and he told me the first month is the hardest. He reassured me that once I become familiar with the prison routines and other inmates, then time would pass much quicker. After two weeks I began to question whether or not I could handle two years in prison. It was a contest unlike any other I had faced before and seemed to have no end or clear path toward victory. I had no choice except to learn how to deal with this and take it one day at a time; another part of my life shaping process. I learned how to slow down and live each day in the moment and focus on the joys and problems happening right now, and that tomorrow will present its own issues and I will be given tools to solve those problems then. I can be stubborn at times, so some lessons were easier to learn than others. My two years in prison gave me plenty of time to kick a lot of my bad habits, and I was forced to be less stubborn.

After 3 months in my first prison location, I was transferred to another prison in West Virginia. The Bureau of Prison's built a brand new U. S. Penitentiary, a woman's maximum security prison, and a minimum security men's prison on a plot of land on top of a mountain in that state. They were looking for inmates they felt could be responsible and trusted enough to move to a lower security prison. Fortunately, I was one of the inmates selected and relocated. This facility was built to house 120 men, but because the prison system is so overcrowded, they packed 180 inmates into this building. There was one building designed barracks style to house us, and another smaller building used for the cafeteria, visiting, and classrooms. This complex was significantly smaller then my last one. The other prison had over 1400 inmates, so I welcomed the change to a much more manageable environment. One of the drawbacks of a smaller facility was there was almost nothing to do. Because this prison was brand new, the entire system had to be built from scratch, and we all felt the initial growing pains.

This actually worked in my favor though. I was bored at the other prison and had a hard time finding activities to stay busy. Now I could use my entrepreneurial skills and passions to create new classes and activities for other inmates. I became an adult continuing education instructor, a GED instructor, and a physical fitness instructor. I was responsible for the class material and content, and I discovered a passion for teaching. It was amazing for me to watch the faces of these guys light up as they felt valued and could grow as individuals. Most of them were told they would never amount to anything in life and were worthless. They had lost all their self confidence and belief in themselves. I was able to stir their passions and be blessed to watch their transformations into men filled with a sense of purpose and desire to improve their own lives. It was truly incredible to watch! I gained so much from the men I was able to interact with every day, they helped me realize how important life can become when we help each other without any agendas or ulterior motives.

When I started my prison sentence, I thought I would just stick to myself and bide my time until it was done, then return home and start life over again. I had no idea these two years would be filled with so many life shaping events and opportunities for me to grow as a man. Without a doubt in my mind, those two years gave me the perfect opportunity to completely strip away all my layers, recognize all the mistakes I made, all the misguided beliefs I had about true happiness, dig deeper and ask the really hard questions of myself, and slowly begin the difficult process of becoming a better man. Prison was the only place I could escape everything and be forced into real personal change. I am so thankful God allowed me the chance to ask for forgiveness and receive it, and He gave me another chance to live life. I was finally starting to "get it".

My faith grew in prison far beyond my own comprehension. I thought I knew Jesus Christ before and held him in my heart, but nothing could be further from the truth. Without question I placed money before God and worshipped it like a false idol. I am forever ashamed of my actions and thoughts. I walked many nights alone, only to discover I was never alone; the Lord was with me talking to me, shaping me, carrying me, and supporting me in my darkest hour. I know some people will call this part of my life a cliché, "He went to prison and found God. I have heard this story before." But, the fact of the matter is, we all have our own journey of discovery and hopefully we all find solace in the Lord and receive His love at some point in our lives before we die. I am not here to convince anyone of anything; what happened is between the Lord and me. Nobody else is involved. However, I would love to share my story if it helps another person grow closer to Him, but I am not here to force it down their throats either. I have been blessed after every speech given by someone coming up to me and stating they see the Lord's hand in my work today, or how touched they were for sharing how I lost my way and how He found me again. They realized how important Jesus is and my story reminded them of the impact God has on our lives and the insignificance of material items. I am so blessed to meet so many amazing people who come up to me to share their own story and journey back into the arms of the Lord. I pray before every speech, "Lord please let me speak Your words and not mine. Let me be in Your service and help someone in the audience today; I do not need to know who it is, just let them hear what You have to say."

As I walked alone in my discovery of the Lord, I witnessed many amazing moments of peace. I remember witnessing love from the simplest things and noticing sights that only He could produce. I felt like I was in a terrible environment, yet I found peace and love the more I opened my own heart and let Him in. I prayed many, many times every day and cried some nights as I walked alone with the pain I felt deep within my own heart for my selfish acts. The Lord allowed me to be broken down knowing how far I needed to fall before He would rescue me and build me back up. I am so thankful for this journey He allowed me to take; my life was incomplete before, but now it is heading in the right direction and I am growing closer to Him every day.

Chapter 8:
Let the transformation begin

When I began my personal mission of discovery, I knew I first needed to honestly recognize my own faults and mistakes and admit to the misery I caused many individuals. I also needed to take responsibility for my actions and feel the pain and realize the consequences. This was not very easy, and it took many long, hard hours of self-conversation and contemplation.

One of the benefits of living at the smaller facility was the freedom to walk outside during designated hours. (There was still a fence around the grounds and many restrictions though.) My work shift ended at 3:30, we had count time at 4:00 p.m, dinner was 4:45, and then the rest of the evening was mine until 9:00 p.m.

I spent countless hours walking by myself. Every day I walked at least 2 hours in a grassy area directly in front of the housing building. This was a relatively small area, but at least it was outside. I typically walked 8-10 miles each night on a weekday in a four hour period, and was able to log 15-20 miles on a weekend day. My boots and shoes were worn out very quickly because I spent so much time on my feet. This was the solitude I needed though, those walks allowed me to escape into my own world and temporarily forget where I was and focus on the changes I needed to make in my life. Within the prison buildings there is a tremendous amount of noise and there is nothing soft to absorb the sound. The floors are concrete, the walls are block, the beds are steel, and the tables are metal. Every little sound is magnified. Plus, there were 180 guys trying to carry on multiple conversations and lockers banging all the time. I could not wait to go outside and escape that racket!

I created my own oval as I walked, and eventually wore the grass down until I had a dirt path. (Humbly, when I finished serving my sentence, the day I was leaving the other guys told me they nicknamed the trail "The Borbi Path". It was a nice tribute for all the thousands of miles I walked.) It did not matter what the weather conditions were, I walked every single night, unless we were in a lockdown and I was not allowed to go outside. When it was winter and the wind was howling on that mountain top and it was 5 degrees outside, I walked; when we faced a blizzard and I could barely see in front of me, I walked; when the summer rolled around and it was hot and humid, I walked; when it was pouring rain and water streamed down my face, I walked; and when it was a perfect day, I walked. This was my therapy and my sessions for healing for me. The drive and determination I used previously to become an advisor was now being used in a positive way to force me to not give up. It instilled energy, focus, and hope for a brighter future. I knew the only person who could change me, was me. I had to do this on my own, but I also had to truly want it. I could not fake this, it had to be real. I would only be fooling myself and would end up failing at some point which would return me right back to the beginning where I would have to start all over again if I did not devote 100% of my attention and energy toward this.

Do you ever experience brief moments of peace? Are there times when you sit on a bench and look at the park or on a dock and gaze out at the water and feel like you are the only person there? Or, when you hike through a trail and listen to the sounds of everything around you, do you escape into your own world free from stress and worry? I was able to experience that almost every day when I walked. I allowed myself to seek out this peace and discover it in many forms. We need to give ourselves permission to find this peace, otherwise it will be right in front of our eyes, yet our blinders may be strapped on so tightly we won't see it. Take a moment every day to seek out this perfect place, but be open to its ever-changing form. I remember looking at the sunset and watching amazing colors in the sky change and create beauty that is indescribable; having a dragonfly land on my hand and admire its vibrant color and body shape; walk at night and watch the constellations become brighter and take shape as the sky grew darker; admire the peacefulness of a deep fog as it created perfect silence while I walked in it; watch a distant thunderstorm build with tremendous power, and then pass leaving a spectacular, perfect double rainbow; and make a wish as a shooting star crossed the night's sky. Here I was, in one of the harshest environments which was designed to break my soul, and be stripped of all the things I clanged to in my previous days, now experiencing peace, a passion for life, and a sense of purpose; how can this be? A person does not come to prison to experience all of this; something is wrong. I don't know how it happened, but somehow God opened my heart and let me witness the amazing world that existed right in front of me. It did not matter where I was, I learned there was beauty in everything - I just had to open my eyes and look. (I don't want to make prison sound like it is a perfect place, because it is not. I still faced many hours of pain, frustration, boredom, and mental anguish while serving my time. I was definitely being punished behind those walls.)

Imagine if you were forced to spend at least 2 hours every day in personal isolation; you could not watch television, answer your phone, surf the net, spend time with your family, or any of the routine things you do on any given day. If you were forced to spend it looking within yourself and mentally discovering what made you tick, then you would learn a lot about your passions and realize your shortfalls. I was given that chance for two years. Trust me, I allowed this to become an opportunity of a lifetime and used my time wisely. Every-day responsibilities do not allow many of us to take two hours and escape, it is almost impossible to do that in today's society, but maybe you could create 30 minutes of private time devoted solely toward growing as a person. Try this, stick with it, and see how you change as a person and learn to look at things differently. See if your stresses and issues suddenly become nonexistent or significantly smaller; you begin to realize what is important in your life and gravitate toward those areas/individuals and reduce the time you spend on nonproductive issues. This does not solve all of your problems, but it will help you gain a new perspective and look at life in a healthier light.

Every day when I walked I asked myself, "Why did you commit those crimes? Why did you steal from those people? Why did you destroy your life?" Of course, there were many more questions I asked, and the more questions I answered, the more questions I had to ask. The good thing was, I am the only person who could answer those questions; I could not defer them to someone else. I walked in silence and waited for my mind to discover the solutions and open new paths of thoughts and focus. I learned and grew every day, not always in the right direction either. I still made mistakes back then, as I do today; I fall on my face often, but I pick myself up, and hopefully learn so I will not repeat the same mistakes. I believe life is about transitional experiences; each experience allows us to move in a new direction, and the information we gain helps us become wiser and live with more passion and balance. I definitely do not have life figured out. I have a long way to go and many tough lessons yet to be learned, but I can say I sleep in peace now and wake with a smile on my face every morning.

In prison, however, as each day passed I allowed myself to go through the process of being broken first; I knew if I did not strip all the "bad" layers away, then I would only be rebuilding my life on a weak foundation that would eventually fail me again one day. This process is easy in theory or when it is happening to someone else, but it was much more difficult when I had to do it by myself and be brutally honest with myself. I was blessed to be surrounded by some incredible men who were good listeners and shared their wisdom and philosophies as well. I was placed in an environment that fostered mental and emotional growth and gave me the chance to ponder my life every day. The conversations I had with these men would last for hours sometimes and I never wanted them to end. I never realized what I was missing in life until I started to ask questions and seek a better understanding of what it meant to be truly happy and at peace. I gained an education on how to live life with balance and a sense of purpose. We discussed all topics and explored many new ways of thinking. I always tried to keep an open mind toward other view points, and encouraged lively debates. (I want to thank David Burry, the gentleman I shared space with for almost two years in prison, for everything he did for me. David was truly a gift from God as he opened his kind heart and helped shape me from the arrogant self-serving individual I was when I entered prison into a man filled with humility and a desire to serve others around me. David was a very patient listener and guided me through many difficult times as I struggled to find myself, and he always knew the perfect words to say that made understanding life so much easier for me. He shared his wisdom with me and never judged me. I am forever grateful for his kindness and support when I lost my way and he brought me back to reality and showed me how to enjoy life again. Thanks to you David; Forever in Christ.)

My time was also spent reading books at night to stimulate my mind. I feel so fortunate to have had many avenues at my disposal, so I was never bored in my quest for personal advancement and development. I benefited from my alone time when I walked, my conversations with other men, and my intellectual gains through reading. From a personal growth point, the two years in prison served a very important purpose. It was the only place I could be stripped of everything and be forced to take an honest look at myself and discover all the mistakes I made and the areas in my life that needed "fixing." I am not saying I want to go back to prison, but it was a time in my life that allowed me to become a better man in all capacities; I learned how to become a better husband, father, son, uncle, brother, and friend to those individuals around me. I thank God every day for giving me the opportunity to be shaped and grow in ways that far exceeded anything I ever dreamed possible. (Of course I missed my family and wanted to be free from prison, but the short term sacrifices are producing long term changes that allow me to be a contributor to society now, not a detractor.)

As I completed my 30 month sentence in prison, I realized where my life had been, but I did not know where it was going. Strangely, that was okay with me, as I finally realized it was more important to live in the present and the future would take care of itself. (It is important to plan for the future. I was just always consumed with the future before, and now I could let that part go.) I did not want to have any part of my previous life and wished for a fresh start. I was sent to a halfway house in a very rough part of downtown Detroit to begin serving the last 3 months of my sentence, as a transitional period back into society. I was divorced the first day I returned to the halfway house; we both knew that was going to happen. We had grown apart and wanted different things out of life now; this was the best move for both of us and continued my process of starting over and discovering a new path in life. I had $50 in my pocket and needed to rebuild my entire life again. I started my painting company again and began building that business to provide an income and means to afford the basic necessities such as food and transportation. I can't explain how overwhelmed with joy I was to be experiencing life outside of those prison walls; every day brought new meaning to my life and allowed me to be thankful for a second chance at life.

Although my life had many amazing aspects to it, I also had to be a realist about it. My life had its own share of immense struggles and sufferings as well. My personal income would fluctuate greatly, and there were weeks when I had zero income and could not afford to buy food. As time passed, I could no longer afford my house payment and lost it to foreclosure. In my first two years of Christmas celebrations with my children, I did not have enough money to buy them any presents, (this broke my heart and I cried). I saved returnable bottles in my garage as my emergency reserve food fund when I had no more money. My heat and electricity were turned off over a short period during the winter months. (My television did not work and I had to tell my children they could not watch their favorite cartoon. I gave them an extra blanket because the house was so cold, and I felt crushed as a father who continued to fail his children and could not provide for their means. I showered them with love and we had many great personal memories together, but that was all I could give them). I was not allowed to have any available credit while I was on probation, so I had to learn how to live with what I had and could not afford health insurance some months. Some weeks I had $20 and needed to figure out how I was going to buy gas for my car so I could drive to work and take my children to school, or determine how little amount of food I absolutely had to buy for my family. I was accustomed to suffering in prison, but that was okay because it only affected me. Now that my children were involved, I felt terrible. I was very happy to have my freedom back, but I did not have any other basic items in my life, and I certainly did not have any luxuries. I could not afford to go to the movies or do any of the things I did prior to my incarceration. My life was the complete opposite from years past, and some days felt worse than in prison. At least in prison I had food and heat provided.

This was a true test personally for me to see if all the changes I claimed to have made were really permanent. Could I avoid falling back into the dark side of greed and lust for money? Would I dabble in it a little just to get back on my feet and then quit before it consumed me again? I am happy to say all the suffering I went through only made me more committed to living this new lifestyle and I would not be tempted. I stayed the course and realized all I was missing was just "stuff." I still had my love for my children, and my faith in God was strong. My desire to lead by example and show we could persevere and come out of this one day soon was filling me with a willingness to survive. It has been a long recovery, and I am still falling short financially some months, but as each day passes, things are getting better and my outlook becomes brighter. I am heading in the right direction and I will be patient as life teaches me to enjoy what I am given at this moment.

Chapter 9:
Life in prison

There are endless prison stories I have and the environment I endured for two years is unique to say the least. Let me share with you some aspects of my prison life.

The clothing I wore was very uncomfortable and exactly the same every day. The pants were dark green, stiff, and provided no comfort at all; I could not wait until my work day was done so I could change into my sweats and be able to bend my legs again. The shirts are the same color green and are very scratchy and stiff as well. My name and prison ID were attached via a patch along the pockets. There are no zippers, and every item of clothing has buttons. I could not wait to get home and put on a pair of jeans! Wearing the same thing every day was mundane and boring to say the least. My days of custom made clothing were long gone; my fashion life had swung to the complete opposite end of the spectrum.

There are no scissors in prison. This presents a big problem when needing a haircut. The inmates who held the position of barber were required to use beard trimmers and combs to cut hair. Many of the men changed their hairstyles in prison and either wore their hair very short, crew cut style, or rarely had their hair cut and grew it very long. Just another example of something you may take for granted in your daily life that was dramatically different for me. The first time I had my hair cut after I was released from prison was funny. The stylist cutting my hair kept looking at my hair in a strange way. I could tell she wondered where the last place was I had my hair cut and who butchered my hair? She finally asked where I had my last hair cut. I answered, in prison. The look on her face was shock and disbelief. I imagine that was the first time she ever heard that answer.

Without being offensive, I quickly need to point out another area that was very challenging to adapt to - bathrooms. There were 8 stalls available for use in a prison housing 180 men. You can imagine how gross and nasty those areas became on any given day. There were also 8 sinks available. Those sinks were clogged all the time because there was no area for guys to wash their dishes if they made food in the housing unit, so they left food remnants in the sink. It was disgusting when I tried to brush my teeth in a sink riddled with little food bits, razor stubble, hair, and old tooth paste from other men. You get the picture of what I faced every morning and evening. I personally today always keep my sink area clean and am thankful for having my own space. Another item I took for granted was looking at a clear image of myself, in prison there are no mirrors. All we had were polished metal squares bolted to the walls. These plates would become scratched from inmates trying to wipe them clean. Try shaving when all you see is a blurry image of your hand swiping along your face. The first time I looked at my reflection in a mirror I was amazed at how much I missed it. (Not in a narcissistic way.)

The cafeteria had its own challenges too. A menu was printed each week, but that did not ensure this was the item served. Plus, it may say, "hamburger," but it did not resemble any hamburger I was familiar with. The prison system had a budget of $1.69 to feed me breakfast, lunch, and dinner; you can imagine the quality of food I was given. It resembled dog food. The menu repeated itself often and most weeks we ate the exact same thing. There were often times when I did not eat the food thrown on my tray, as I physically could not force myself to eat that slop. We had a salad offering every day, but the lettuce was brown, wilted, and often slimy, and there were no vegetables. It was only lettuce and watered down dressings which tasted awful. The vegetables designated for the salad were stolen by the kitchen inmates and sold on the black market to other inmates in the housing unit. The best meal of the day was breakfast because it was plain cheerio's and milk. It is hard to screw that up.

Our choices for beverages were coffee, milk, and water. I heard coffee was being removed from the menu soon from budget cuts. The only utensil available to eat with was a bright orange plastic spork; try cutting a piece of meat with a spork that broke often. There were many meals I had to pick the item up with my hands and eat it like a caveman.

Inmates would line up for chow at least 15 minutes in advance because the individuals who were last often did not receive a full meal. Inmates would steal some of the mainline food and try to sell it on the black market to others who wanted more to eat than what was allotted them at the meal. (Why an inmate wanted more of that slop was beyond my comprehension, but some guys liked the food.)

I do have to give them some credit though. On Christmas and Easter we were fed a holiday meal which was quite tasty by prison standards. Usually food was donated by a local business so we could enjoy a different type of meal. One event we ate half a chicken, broccoli, bag of chips, and pecan pie for dessert. That was a real treat for all of us. The bag of chips was one year past the expiration date, but it was still the best bag of chips I ever ate! This gave me the chance to appreciate food so much more now. When I had all that money I ate at many gourmet restaurants and tasted food that was prepared perfectly, yet I always took it for granted and never appreciated what I was eating. That has all changed now. I eat a peanut butter and jelly sandwich and I am loving life. It is the simple meals I enjoy the most now; I learned to be thankful for every meal I eat and savor food in a whole new way.

I have endless food stories, but I think you get the picture about how bad it was inside prison.

The living area I shared with another man was 40 square feet. Imagine coming home from your workday and attempting to relax in such a small area. And, don't forget, the other inmate is trying to find space to relax as well; we were crammed to say the least. The lockers were very small and contained my clothing, books, personal items, and any food I purchased for the week. It helped me live with only the items I needed. There was no room for excess in my life anymore. This was another great lesson for me to learn and change from my previous life.

I slept on the top bunk. My mattress was 1 ½ inches thick and just a little wider than my own body. I did not have a pillow, and we were issued two very thin blankets and scratchy sheets. I froze most nights. The building was all open and there were no dividers between us, so I could hear every sound in that building. There were many nights I barely slept because of all the snoring; I could hear the guy rolling in his bed 20 feet away from me. It was terrible. There was absolutely no privacy nor place to find peace or "escape." I gained a new respect for being alone, but I also learned how to get along in a crowded environment and have respect for another man's space too. I never imagined how tough living under those conditions would be, but being placed there forced me to adjust, adapt, and accept what I was given. These are life lessons I still use today.

I had to do my own laundry and share 3 machines with the entire population. I was fortunate my job was close to the living quarters, so I could do my laundry during the day when it was less crowded. Some inmates did their laundry in the middle of the night because that was the only available time for them. One of the golden rules in prison was you never touched another man's items/stuff! This created a problem when a person left his laundry in the machine and forgot about it; he clogged the system while other guys were waiting to use the machine. I saw fights break out because another inmate moved clothing out of a machine to do his own laundry; that was a no - no.

Of course there were numerous surprise shakedowns to control the illegal items in the prison. I was surprised most of the time the guards did a good job of sneaking up on the inmates. I would be lying in my bed when all of the sudden 20 guards would storm into the building and tell everyone to leave immediately as they escorted inmates outside. Guys would scatter and attempt to throw items into the trash can if they made it that far. The guards knew how the game was played and ran to the cans quickly as well. There were only two doors leading in/out of the building, so we were all searched as we left the building. At that point the guards would tear the place apart looking for cell phones, cigarettes, alcohol, and drugs. We had to wait outside until they said it was clear to return. It did not matter what the weather conditions were outside either. One time we waited in the pouring rain as they took two hours to shake us down. The funny thing was, the inmates who controlled the black market were pretty smart and knew where to hide items in places the guards would never look. They would never hold the items or be linked in any way. Sometimes there was a tip and the guards raided a specific locker or living area; I saw guys get packed up and shipped to another facility all the time.

I remember walking at night and passing two inmates sitting on a bench talking on a cell phone; at that time cell phones were considered a serious security risk and extra time was added to an inmate's sentence if he was caught.

The black market was very well run and lucrative for the guys in charge. One of the "leaders" had a birthday party and somehow arranged to have shrimp cocktail, fruit salad, and champagne for his party! I was blown away by their bold behavior. They asked if I wanted some, but I was not willing to risk getting caught and be shipped to another facility or have more time added to my sentence. I already learned my lessons and was not willing to cross that line. Most of the time inmates wanted basic items, such as good coffee, razors, an mp3 player, and muscle protein powder, harmless items meant to provide simple comforts to help the days pass. I was shaken down by the guards often because they knew I walked all the time and was a likely suspect to gather contraband left on the grounds. (For the record, I never involved myself in that kind of activity; I just wanted to be left alone to walk with my own thoughts.)

Visitation presented its own set of frustrations and benefits. Some individuals did not want to visit me because they were scared of being on prison property and did not know what to expect. I understood this and respected their decisions. I always appreciated all of my visits, but never forced anyone to come to a place that made them uncomfortable. My children visited me about every other month. This became one of the things I loved most, yet also the time I was frustrated most. My children were very young when I went to prison, ages 3 & 5, so they did not fully comprehend what prison meant and represented. This became a very hard discussion and explanation when they visited. They started to recognize the routines and knew what to expect with each visit. The waiting room was fairly small and housed 60-70 people at a time; the chairs were all in a row, similar to airport seating. Once again there was nothing "soft" to absorb sound in this room, so as the room filled up, it became almost impossible to carry on a conversation without yelling in each other's ear. It was not conducive when more than one person came to visit because I could not move my chair to sit across from everyone. We all sat in a row, so I had to speak around someone to carry on a conversation with multiple people. Plus, the chairs were hard molded plastic and very uncomfortable to sit in for long periods of time. I give a lot of credit to the individuals who came to visit me. They had to put up with a lot just to say hello to me. I am thankful for their efforts and many sacrifices.

When my children visited, they were checked in by an adult, and then waited for my name to be called. I knew when they were coming and waited outside of the inmate door. I walked into the shakedown area to be patted down by the guard before he cleared me to enter the visiting room. My children knew this routine and waited on the other side of this heavy steel door. When the door swung open I walked through and they would run and jump into my arms! It brought a tear to my eye every single time I held them, and I gave them the biggest hug I possibly could. It warmed my heart and allowed me to escape prison in my own mind for a few hours. Words can't describe the joy I felt and how much that moment meant to me as their father. The rest of the visiting time was spent holding them on my lap as we laughed, or sitting on the floor as we played a game. I could not get enough of their smiles and hugs. I received the biggest emotional high from these shared moments and never wanted them to end. But, I knew I could not stop time, and with each passing minute their departure grew closer and closer. I had to learn to live in the moment and enjoy their time and not worry about the future. If I worried, then this would detract from my joy of the moment and rob me of why they were there in the first place. So, I focused on every second with them and faced their goodbyes when it happened later. My heart was broken every time they left. They would ask me, "Daddy, I want you to come home with us today." "I want you to be at my birthday party next week." "Can you tuck me into bed tonight?" "When are you coming home? I want to cuddle with you on the couch and watch tv." "I don't like it when I wake up and you are not there in the morning." I was so sad every time they left as I watched them cry, because their wish of leaving with their father was not coming true. They always arrived with hope that this visit would be different and maybe I would walk through the door carrying them as we drove home together, but each time they had to leave with their own broken heart knowing I was staying behind. As a parent you can relate and feel our pain.

I spent two years wondering, "What are my children doing at this very moment? Are they hurt? Are they smiling? Who are they playing with? What made them laugh today? What did they learn today?" I have nobody to blame except myself; I committed the crime and needed to face the consequences of my actions and deal with the punishments accordingly. I was willing to do that, but I did not think it was fair for my children to have to suffer for my failures. They did not deserve to be subjected to those pains.

This time away from them taught me how precious their time is and how much I valued their love. I tell my children every day I see them how much I love them and how proud I am to be their father. We take that for granted, and most parents become consumed with their own daily routines that they forget to love their children and show it. Most parents would do anything for their child, but never take action to demonstrate that love. Give your child a hug today, or tell them how important they are to you and watch their hearts fill with emotion. I don't want to have my life suddenly cut short and not be given the opportunity to tell my children how I truly feel about them; I want them to know they are loved and I valued every moment we shared together.

Among the difficulties I faced in prison were dealing with the "power trips" from the younger guards. During one visit on a Saturday morning, a show of control was given. Every Saturday morning, around 10:30 am, there is an official count and the guards have to report the inmates names and ID's to the central office. There were four inmates in the visiting room including myself. The guard typically calls in the information about the inmates and does not disrupt the visitation. But, this young guard wanted to show his power. He stood up and yelled in a very authoritative voice, "Count time! Everyone against the wall!"

As an inmate I am required to immediately stop what I am doing, walk over to the wall closest to his station, stand in line with the other inmates, state my name and prison ID number, hold my ID card in front of me, and remain silent until the guard announces count is cleared. That guard intimidated everyone in that room, he wanted to show, that may be your father, brother, uncle, son, or friend, but I just demonstrated to you how "I own this man." He has to do what I tell him to do, and without any questions or hesitations he has to follow my orders. There were some children playing with their father and they were freaked out by this scene. I was fortunate my brother was the only person visiting me, and he knew about these types of abuses. He had already witnessed things like this before. I was treated like a second class citizen most of the time in prison, but this helped teach me how to become a humble man and recognize it was not important to be viewed as "important." I learned how to value myself and not seek the approval of others to feel "important."

I do have a funny story about one visit from my brother. I am very fortunate to have a tremendous relationship with my twin brother, and he came to visit me every single month while I was away. This was a huge sacrifice he made for me. It cost him money, personal drive time, and time away from his own family to be with me and make me laugh. We shared hours of conversation about every topic, and he helped make my time in prison manageable. He was always the first person to arrive when the visiting opened on Friday evenings, and stayed until the last minute when they kicked him out. One Friday evening when he was leaving, the guard noticed we were twins. This guard knew me to be an inmate without problems or cause for concern. The guard smiled and said, "I noticed you guys are twins and look alike; I don't care which one of you goes back there, (meaning back to the prison housing unit), as long as one of you is around for count time." My brother and I laughed. At that moment in my sentence I would have loved to "escape" for a night and sleep in a normal bed and eat a normal meal;

that would have been heaven for me! Having my brother stay in prison overnight would have been an eye opening experience for him as well. He knew about most of the friends I had in prison and they said they would have gladly helped him follow protocol and been unnoticed by the guards. But, neither one of us was willing to take that risk. I did not want any more time added to my sentence if I was caught, and with my brother's luck the prison would have gone into a lockdown and he may have been stuck there for a week. Try explaining that to his wife! But, it still provided a little humor for both of us to think of the "what if" scenario.

Karl, my brother, always mailed me any kind of information I requested, sent me money if I needed it, and made sure I had everything I could legally possess while in prison. He never balked or told me no; he just took care of it. I will always be grateful for his efforts and everything he did for me. The hours he spent with me during visiting always passed like minutes. I realize this was not the first place he wanted to be, but he made it all happen and never complained about any of it.

There was one thing I loved about every visit I had, no matter who was visiting me - the food. I realize most people will think I am crazy, but the vending machine food was something I looked forward to every time. I absolutely could not wait to have a soda, candy bar, and main food item from the machine!! This was a huge treat for me and I felt like it was my birthday every time someone rolled out the quarters and bought my food. I was not allowed to handle money, so the visitor had to go to the machine and deposit the coins, and then I would stare at the machine and determine which item I wanted as my mouth began to salivate. I am not kidding - the nasty hamburger or sandwich you see in the vending machines that you say to yourself, "who would eat that awful thing?" is what I craved. Sometimes I would set the food down next to me and say a prayer being thankful for this gift I was given before I absolutely devoured it. It was yet another lesson I learned about being grateful for all I had, but this could only be taught to me after I lost everything. Who would have thought a simple can of soda and a candy bar would become so valued to me?

The visits I received and valued from everyone gave me a chance to mentally escape prison for a short period and helped me realize that my stay there was only temporary. But, once my visitor left the room, reality quickly returned and I was shocked back into the prison life. When I left the prison waiting room, I had to pass through a shakedown area. After each visit, a guard would pat me down, and then require me to endure a humiliating strip search to make sure I did not hide any contraband or attempt to smuggle anything back into the compound. This was very dehumanizing and always made me feel like a true convict, like I was the second class citizen the guards wanted me to become. Standing there naked and being put through a routine of moves and "exposures" to leave no doubt I did not have anything on or in my body was a terrible experience to say the least. Some inmates requested no visitors, simply because they did not want to go through this traumatic process. For me it was a price I had to pay to have some connection with the outside world. I needed to see my friends and family, so this was just another part of the process.

Dealing with the staff and guards was definitely challenging. There were two extremes with the guards. On one side I had to deal with the young 23 year old who never held power before and did not know how to use it, so he became obsessed with it and realized he could basically force me to do whatever he wanted and I could not say anything about it. This was difficult for inmates who held power within the prison system. They had to find a balance between maintaining respect from their fellow prisoners and not pushing the guards too much to get themselves thrown into solitary confinement. These young guards were very focused on maintaining every rule they learned from basic training, and did not recognize it was impossible to enforce all of these rules. They definitely needed exposure to the prison system to soften up and discover which battles were worth fighting the inmates on and which were better left alone.

I remember being stopped as I was walking through the hallway and patted down for anything illegal. This was ridiculous and a complete waste of both of our times. They would do impromptu locker inspections as well. These guards were constantly walking through the housing unit and would stop, open my locker, and take most of my items out to verify I did not possess anything illegal, then I would have to climb down off my bed and clean up the mess he created and put everything back. It was a hassle to say the least, and the guard would be ridiculed by the inmates when he did that. An inmate would yell from across the unit, "Go back to your office where you belong. Leave us alone."

The other extreme came from the seasoned guards who had been in the system for 20+ years. These guards were more concerned about doing as little as possible while maintaining their "easy" money paychecks. There were times when the prison was short staffed and we had one guard monitoring the entire unit. We would only see this guard during count times. One Saturday he did a mandatory count first thing in the morning and then announced to the entire unit he would make a deal with us. He would stay in the front office and leave us alone until his next count at 4:00, but we had to manage ourselves and not get into any fights or do anything to make him look bad. This was a win/win. He sat in a chair all day watching tv, and was paid for doing absolutely nothing, while the inmates had the freedom to play cards, roll dice and gamble, cook meals using stolen food, listen to their music on illegal mp3 players, and live a quasi normal life for a few hours without always looking over their shoulder watching for a guard to sneak up on them. We all liked the veteran guards because we knew what we were dealing with and it allowed us a sense of freedom. The senior inmates basically told the new inmates to not screw things up for the rest of us or there would be serious consequences. The black market controllers used these times to bring in their "merchandise" and replenish their stock.

This black market needed to exist, and it was healthy for the system to function. It helped inmates maintain a sense of normalcy and not feel deprived of everything they ever owned previously. It kept inmates from becoming so frustrated that they would get violent or act out against the guards or other inmates. Ironically, this helped things run smoother and was a necessary evil in the eyes of the prison senior staff and guards. No prison staff will admit this market exists, but they know the prison has fewer problems when this is controlled and managed properly by select inmates. The key was making sure it did not get out of hand. For example, if half of the inmate population had cell phones, then that would not be good for anyone. I was fortunate to be in a prison where basically anything was available on this black market, but I did not witness the inmates abuse it either.

One of the crazier stories I have was when a couple of inmates took things to the extreme and left the compound to fulfill a "personal" need. As I mentioned, anything can be arranged within this market. If you have a larger ticket item request, then a banking system exists where if you wanted something, then you would have someone you know send money to a specific contact known to the operator of the black market. Once that person verifies the money has been deposited and accepted, then your "item" would be delivered. These inmates had been in the system a long time, and decided they wanted to connect with some prostitutes. So, the arrangements were made. They escaped the prison grounds and were hiding behind a hill so the guards could not see them, then a car pulled up and picked them up, they drove down the mountain to a local hotel, "completed their personal business," and were returned to the prison location without ever being discovered. Needless to say, this was a very brazen and foolish act in my opinion.

They took a very high risk, but in their mind it was warranted and worth it.

Being the fitness instructor offered some challenges in prison too. The facility I was at did not offer any fitness equipment and attempted to prevent inmates from strength training. I needed to be creative and designed routines based on core strength, increased agility and balance, and creative ways to build muscle. This was a new way of thinking to most inmates, and I had to do some convincing to get guys to attend my first class. However, when they started feeling the changes and realized it was much harder than it looked, I had no problem filling my other classes. Inmates always found ways to build muscle. They did pull-ups using the cross bar supports in the showers, filled their laundry bags with books and makeshift water bottles, and did a lot of push-ups.

In the final fitness class I taught before I completed serving my sentence, I changed things up a little. One of the guys from the landscape department was able to find small and medium sized rocks all over the prison grounds, so I had him deliver them to a corner of the fence area and we used those as weights in the class. Once again, this was another way we needed to be creative and make use of what was available. It was not easy holding those rocks, but I will always remember those routines and the fun we had.

This is another example of the strange logic that exists in prison. The inmate who bunked a row from me was always sleeping. He slept in until the last minute before he had work call, and then slept after his work day was completed for the rest of the night. One day I asked him why he spent so much time in bed asleep. His answer was, "If I spend 12 hours sleeping, then I am only serving half of my time." I smiled and laughed, but it was hard for me to argue his logic. Individuals find their own ways to pass their time.

I was fortunate to learn many hard lessons while in prison and be exposed to an environment unlike any other. For most individuals it is hard to imagine losing personal freedom, but let me assure you it is a very important aspect of life and it greatly affects one's emotional state. In prison I was told what to do and when to do it. The sooner I accepted this rule, the easier my life would become.

There are too many stories to tell about prison. The main point is that it was a place for me to escape society for two years, remove layers of wrong choices and rebuild my life. I came away a new man and one with renewed interest in morals, ethics, values, and determination to lead a balanced life filled with passion again.

My first two things I wanted to do when I left prison were. One, take off my shoes and walk on carpeting, and take a shower by myself. In prison every surface is "hard" and I was required to wear shoes at all times. When I walked on carpet and felt the soft fibers under my feet it was amazing! I realize it may be hard for you to relate, but it was something I missed and now appreciate every day. It was also great to not have shower shoes on my feet and finally have some privacy. It is the simple things I missed the most.

Chapter 10:
New Beginnings

I am a father of two wonderful children and am happy to say I lead by example now. I can teach them about the dark side of success and share the life mistakes I already made. I hope to help them make better choices as they grow older. I am blessed to return to them a better man who is thankful for everything and wants to live every day to the fullest extent possible. I can die today without any regrets.

It is amazing how I had to take an event like going to prison, something people can not ever imagine going through, and say those were the best two years of my life. Without those soul searching years I might not have been able to discover who I am and how I can be of service to those around me; I am here to help and learn now.

Life is all about transformations and experiences. I believe there is no such thing as a bad experience; they help shape us and make us who we are today. Please take the opportunity to look at life as a learning experience and change the areas in life you are unhappy with. Don't make the same mistake I did and let your life get so far out of control that drastic measures have to be taken to return it to its intended path.

Looking back, I can still say I would not change a thing about what happened to my own life. I went through some very rough times and had to learn many lessons the hard way, but the reality is I learned those lessons and made the necessary changes to lead a better life.

(If I could go back, I would change the hurt and pain I caused those close to me and the investors I stole money from. I wish the individuals whom were fired and had nothing to do with my crime would not have lost their jobs, and the anguish and sorrow I caused my children during my absence was erased. I personally needed to feel emotional pain from the consequences of my actions and poor decisions, and I deserved that, but all the other people who were affected from my choices did not deserve any of those ill effects.)

I returned to society with an almost insurmountable $1 million dollars of debt, (I owe $750,000 in restitution and $175,000 in back taxes), and a criminal record that most people will forever judge me on. I am a divorced father with two children, living paycheck-to-paycheck, self employed, and struggling to live a "normal" life again. I am living the complete antithesis of my life just a few years back. But, this is just another step in my journey through life and I will take it one day at a time. I have been through many failures in life and never let them get me down. I accepted my mistakes, tried to learn from them, and made changes to not repeat them. Life is full of opportunities and I am in the process of discovering my next high point in life. As I have told others, "Failure is just the first step toward success."

Chapter 11:
Now

I am amazed at how quickly life is moving forward for me. It is hard to believe the 5 year anniversary from my prison release date is fast approaching. I continue to learn every day; some days I fall and make mistakes, while others are spent enjoying life to the fullest.

My life is blessed in so many ways as I grow into a better father, husband, brother, uncle, and son. I am fortunate to have many opportunities to share love and laughter with those closest to me and cherish memories created every single day. However, my financial struggles have not disappeared. I am required to submit annual audited financial statements to the court system which is used to determine my monthly restitution payments. My back tax debt to the IRS looms and has not been resolved, and my personal monthly income still fluctuates and is inconsistent. Many of the difficulties in my life persist as I will never escape the mistakes of my past, but those serve as reminders of the arrogance I once possessed and help keep me grounded in my decision making process going forward.

Personally, I am very happy to say I am in love with a woman who is able to look past all of the mistakes I made in my previous life and allows me to be "me." We are newly married and have begun to share our lives filled with passion for each other and look at each day as an opportunity to grow closer and experience new adventures together. I am blessed the Lord brought into my life a person who helps me grow and keeps me balanced in many ways. She is beautiful inside and out, and I wake with a smile knowing she loves me with an open heart. Tracy's support is very important to me and the wisdom she shares brightens my days in many ways.

Parker and Gracie, my son and daughter, have grown past the days when I was not involved in their daily lives. They enjoy each day as any child their age should, by laughing, smiling, and having fun. Our relationship continues to grow and I am thankful for their love and support. We have talked about the mistakes I made in the past, and they know all about my career as a speaker sharing my message with so many people. I am proud of them and all they do to bring happiness into my life.

I am fortunate to have two wonderful stepchildren, Josh and Dylan, added to my life, and I look forward to watching them grow and discover their own paths toward happiness as their lives progress. I have been given a second chance at life and continue to be rewarded by having so many wonderful people surrounding me.

I have become a full time speaker traveling nationally and internationally sharing my message about the dark side of success. I am humbled to say my story touches thousands of individual lives every year, and I hope I can help at least one person avoid making the same mistakes I made. It is my mission to share the addictions of greed and materialism and how consuming they can become in a person's life.

I feel blessed after every speech when individuals take the time to come up to me after my presentation and shake my hand to tell me their own stories, or just to say thanks for sharing. It is amazing to me when I look into the eyes of another person and witness their sincerity and true inner self.

I meet with my twin brother Karl weekly to maintain and grow our relationship, and sometimes laugh about the visits we had behind those prison walls. My mother continues to be a positive influence for me and supports me in every way; she has seen the best of me and the worst of me, and she never judged me.

I am thankful for all I have and all I receive every day. I still love to walk and experience the fresh air and wonderful sights God leaves for me to discover daily. May you find peace in your own heart each and every day.

Thank you for allowing me to share my story with you.

About the Author

As a speaker, John Borbi has captivated and inspired thousands through his real life story and the extremes he experienced. Because of his life experiences, John is uniquely qualified to share techniques on managing moral and ethical dilemmas. He continues to be consulted by corporations for engaging training and motivates others with amazing workshops.

John travels the country to challenge and educate a diverse group including university students, corporate managers and employees, and is highly sought after for keynote addresses at national and international conferences. Audiences consistently give him the highest ratings and say they left wanting more. John Borbi leaves audiences ready to take action that can lead to profound changes in their personal and professional lives.

Areas of expertise include:

- Inspirational life events speaker
- Corporate ethics consultant
- University student character choices speaker
- Empowering motivational consultant

Learning Points participants will:

- Develop a strategy to manage and achieve success.
- Discover techniques to resolve moral and ethical dilemmas and avoid justifying unethical decisions.
- Experience daily passion for life and avert obsession which guarantees future failure.

Toughlessons.com